THE
ART
OF
DRESSING

THE

Ageless, Timeless, Original Style

ART

OF

DRESSING

TZIPORAH SALAMON

RIZZOLI NEW YORK

New York · Paris · London · Milan

"You gotta have style. it helps you get down the stairs. It helps you get up in the morning. It's a way of life."—Diana Vreeland

STYLE. What is it? Where does it come from? How do we get it? Derived from "stilus," the Latin word for a sharp instrument used to make long-lasting marks on clay or wax writing tablets, style is indeed that lasting impression that stays with you. It's the characteristic or element that is expressed in a unique and consistent matter. It's the image that leaves an indelible mark on the viewer forever.

My own first encounter with style came at an early age. The men and women I grew up with, my parents and numerous aunts and uncles, all Hungarian Holocaust survivors living in the newly formed state of Israel in the early 1950s, possessed it in spades. The women wore dresses, shoes with thick high heels, and red lipstick; the men wore suits or at the very least sports jackets and pants, white shirts, and graphic ties. The clothes fit their bodies like gloves as they were all custom made by either my mother, a dressmaker, or my father, a tailor, and the fabrics were first rate. These Eastern European men and women continued to dress in their newly adopted home—in this small and dusty Mediterranean country in the north of Africa—exactly the way they dressed in the old country. Elegance was the order of the day. Even if there were no roads yet, even if they had to stand on long food ration lines in the summer heat, my mother and aunts donned their

dresses and did not neglect their looks. They had their hair done, they painted their nails, they were ladies. Not to be outdone by their wives, and although they might have had only one summer suit and one winter suit, the men were always properly attired in suit and tie and often a hat. In spite of the casualness of the Israeli society, the intense sun beating down on them, and the still-unpaved terrain, they dressed.

Another huge influence on my impressionable younger self were the clothes and costumes worn by the newly emerging Israeli singers, some of whom were from the Arab world. Shoshana Damari, the "Queen of Hebrew music," a dark-haired Yemenite beauty who wore dangling silver earrings, heavy silver necklaces, and exquisitely embroidered clothes left a permanent mark on my style. Different from the European women in my family, her looks were exotic, artistic, exciting, and aroused in me a curiosity, awakening some ancient deep roots I was to explore years later.

Secretly, I couldn't wait to grow up and join the military, where both boys and girls served from age eighteen. How I admired the beautiful girl soldiers in their snappy, well-fitted army uniforms. They exuded a strength, a toughness, an independence. I coveted their army fatigues with those tight pants or short skirts and well-formed jackets, and especially the caps on their heads. I watched them alongside the road as they were hitching to get to their  destination, taking in their strong bodies, their good looks, and the white polish on their nails. They were my future self.

As my parents sewed all my clothes, I was naturally a well-dressed child from the start. I developed into an equally well-dressed teenager and young adult. But did I have style? And what is the distinction?

I was to learn that lesson in my late twenties when I decided to leave Berkeley, California, where I was pursuing a PhD program in psychology to move back to New York to pursue fashion. It was 1979 and my hippie clothes—big skirts,

(top left)
My mother was not only beautiful and stylish, but an accomplished dress-maker and baker. Here she is in a dress of her own making.

(bottom left)
Uncle Nazo, my father's youngest brother, who lived with us until I was six, riding his bicycle in his custom-made riding coat and knickers that my father made for him.

(opposite)
My father, Izidore Izak Salamon, wearing a suit he made himself.

(below)
My beautiful Aunt Yoli, my father's favorite sister, a seamstress, wearing a suit made by my father.

embroidered blouses, loop earrings, colorful wedge sandals—were not going to serve me in my chosen new profession. A big change in style was called for and I had my work cut out for me.

It was then that I first saw a photo of Nancy Cunard, the writer, heiress, and political activist with her short chic bob haircut, arms laden with ivory bracelets from wrist to elbow. This was style and I wanted it. I cut out the photo and went straight to the hairdresser, where I cut off my long curls. My transformation was underway.

I began exploring the world of fashion, its icons, its influencers, its designers. Coco Chanel became my muse. I particularly loved the casual trousers, the sailor striped T-shirts, the turbans, and the berets. Diana Vreeland, the columnist, editor, and consultant to the Metropolitan Museum's Costume Institute was another role model. I read everything I could find about her, including her autobiography, *D.V.*, and sought out old issues of *Vogue* from when she was editor-in-chief. Her exuberance, her larger-than-life personality, her colorful and imaginative exhibitions at the Met, and the colorful and imaginative spreads in *Vogue* encouraged me to seek my own style and to march to my own drum.

It is precisely this characteristic—originality—that sets one apart and is the key to having style. The only way to get it is by knowing oneself. Style is an inside job, and may take years to achieve. It requires discipline, study, and attention. It starts with having a sense of self, with knowing who you are, where you come from, what attracts you, what turns you on. Style does not just happen; it needs to be cultivated, chiseled, refined.

In the next chapters, you will meet ten women who exemplify style. All are over the age of fifty because it usually

(opposite)
My ode to Charlie Chaplin.

(below)
Wearing a dress I de-
signed that was then
made by a friend.

(right)
Wearing a Matsuda hat,
and a Comme des Garçons
jumper. The scarf was
given to me by a Japanese
man after I complimented
him on it.

takes that long to master this thing called style. All have their distinct looks, their unique style. What they share is a full life, an active life, a life that makes demands of them and to which they give of themselves wholeheartedly. Few of these women are involved in the world of fashion, although some of them are quite fashionable. All of them are stylish, and all of them are triumphantly themselves.

The final chapter explores the elements of design and what it takes to elevate dressing to an art form. Armed with these tools, you will be well-equipped to set out on your own journey—it is one that you must traverse alone, picking up clues and inspirations along the way—which will lead you to finding your own indelible mark to leave upon the world.

TZIPORAH
SALAMON

"At my essence, the core of my being, my one consistent characteristic is that I dress."

from his lips. I felt such beauty and reverence as I looked out at the room filled with men under their black and white striped shawls being transported to another dimension. This was theater, this was drama, this was magic. Then home to a delicious Shabbat meal where my mother's culinary skills, perhaps equal to her sewing talents, were on full display, followed by the customary Shabbat nap. Late afternoon to awake and don a fresh new dress to accompany my father on the Shabbat walk—we promenaded up Herzl Street, the main road, stopping to greet his friends and cronies. My dresses were always greatly admired as the adults looked down at me and smiled. How happy and proud I was to be well dressed and loved.

Among the many wonderful things about growing up in Israel were the holidays. Every one of them was special, with its own flavor, food, and ritual. My favorite was Purim, the holiday in which kids don costumes, celebrating the courageous deeds of Queen Esther, who saved her people from the evil Haman who planned to kill all the Jews in the ancient Persian Empire. For this holiday my mother went all out with my costumes. Her imagination was set free and every year she outdid herself with the planning and execution of my outfits. Over the years I was: an arab girl, Snow White, a Persian princess, Santa Claus, one of the seven dwarfs. One year, for Chanukah, I was a *sufganiah*, a doughnut, one of the traditional foods for the Holiday of Lights. This she made entirely out of brown crepe paper to which she attached a wire so the skirt stood all around me like a hula hoop. With a wide hat, pompoms attached to my white gloves, and rouged cheeks, I indeed looked good enough to eat.

Her outfits were masterpieces—each with its own hat, proper shoes, and correct accessories. Her attention to detail was exemplary and nothing was too difficult for her. Her skilled hands could sew, knit, crotchet, and embroider, and she worked her magic on the toughest fabrics, from fine silk velvets to rough burlap. If needed, my father's tailoring skills were called in, as when he made me the satin knickers that I wore as one of the dwarfs. I was their play doll and could not have been happier with my role.

Another delight, perhaps the greatest one, was my father's tailoring shop, my magic kingdom. Located in the heart of the city, in an alleyway, the shop was well equipped with a huge work table, two sewing machines, bolts of fabrics, two dress forms, an ironing board with a heavy iron, scissors, pins and needles strewn all over the floor, and fashion magazines with beautiful women on the covers wearing well-fitted suits and donning hats, perched at rakish angles. My father's specialty was women's suits, although he had both male and female clients. Dad was generous with his time and allowed me to hang out there as long as I wanted, with me helping by picking up the pins and needles that magically lifted onto the heavy magnet I held to them.

He was proud of his work and always pointed out the fine details of his craft: "Look at the lapels, how they sit just so. Look at how nicely the shoulders fall. Look at the perfect button holes." Even at that tender young age, he was preparing me to know and appreciate fine tailoring, and those lessons remain invaluable. His tailoring shop was the hub for all my parents' friends and relatives. It was where the men gathered

Wearing 1920s men's silk polka-dot pajamas with an Edwardian jacket and a 1930s hat.

after work, stopping to drink a cup of coffee, smoke a cigarette, talk of their day, argue politics, and gossip. I was allowed entry to this man's world, and I loved it. Little Tzippy was the shop's mascot and I observed and absorbed it all.

When it was time for me to go to school, I wore the school uniform, a jumper of blue and white checked cotton with a white blouse underneath. Not wanting to flaunt economic differences, the leaders of the young country thought it best that all schoolchildren wear the same uniform. This in no way diminished my love of clothes or dressing up. After all, there were plenty of opportunities, including every day after school when I rushed home, put on my play clothes, and gathered the neighborhood kids, playing "teacher" to their "students." Or I would put on a fashion show for the relatives, especially on those occasions when a new package had just arrived from America.

In the first grade, in order to prepare for our first book, we were to embroider the cover for it. Our teacher, "Mora Yaffa," which means "Teacher Yaffa," truly lived up to her moniker: "yaffa" means "beautiful" and beautiful she was. Every day, she asked us to take out our brown burlap cover and embroider our names on the front. Girls and boys alike, we were so excited, especially as they told us that we would have a big celebration to which our parents were invited with the school principal handing out our books himself. I, the smartest girl, along with Avi, the smartest boy, were chosen to be the valedictorians. I was busy preparing my speech, while my parents were busy preparing my outfit. They decided that my father would make me a new pair of pants and a white shirt. They chose a masculine look executed by my father rather than a feminine look executed by my mother. I guess they felt that the act of leadership is a masculine one and hence their choice of pants and shirt. My mother did add a white bow to my hair. Along with my sturdy black patent-leather shoes, the bow was a touch of girlishness to this rather male look. The importance of clothes and the appropriateness of the occasion were lessons I learned at a very young age.

Then, when I was nine years old, my mother decided to move the family to America. While both my parents had wanted to immigrate to America from Europe after the war, the American quota kept them out and hence they immigrated to Israel instead. By 1959, when we did move, my father had grown quite fond of living in Israel and his business was thriving, but my mother insisted that with his golden hands surely we could become millionaires in this land of opportunity. A risk-taker and confident in his abilities to secure work, even without speaking the language, my father agreed. In spite of my protests to leave me in Israel with my favorite Uncle Nazo, I boarded the ship bound for New York, where they hoped an easier and richer life awaited. Ever the drama queen, I prostrated myself onto the ground and kissed the earth before walking up to the ship, a scene I must have seen in some movie. When everyone cheered as we caught sight of the Statue of Liberty, the tears rolled down my eyes as the reality of my new homeland sunk in.

My first impression as we pulled into the New York harbor and I saw grey all around me was that the sun did not shine in America—only in Israel. We moved in with my father's

Wearing vintage Yves Saint Laurent pants, a Missoni cap, an Isabela Toledo sweater, a Prada bag, an antique shawl, and sandals from 1959.

Tziporah Salamon

brother in Crown Heights where the first lesson my aunt taught me was red light/green light. There were no traffic lights in Israel, not to mention hardly any cars in our little town. This was a different story; Brooklyn was busy, bustling, fast, dangerous. "Why did you leave the Garden of Eden and come to Hell?" I demanded of my mother. And hell it was, starting with my name. My teacher, who never heard of "Tziporah," decided it was spelled C-i-p-o-r-a and showed me how to write it. I came to dread going to school. Where once I was the top of my class, I was now the class dummy. There was a committee to help me learn English and I felt humiliated. What's worse, the kids could not pronounce my name, laughed at my accent, and ridiculed my clothes.

Two years of this was all I could stand. In the middle of the 6th grade, I decided to change my name. I needed a new name, an American name; I was sure that would change everything. Being a studious child, I made a study: the most popular girls' names in the U.S. in 1962 were "Linda" and "Susan." Yet these were a bit too ordinary for me; I wanted to stand out, be sophisticated. I narrowed it down to "Lynn" and "Sue." Then, I realized that the most popular girl in school was named "Lynn Turkel." That was it. I changed my name to Lynn; I was twelve years old and my priority was popularity, not individual identity. At the same time, I came home and announced to my parents that I no longer wanted their "homemade clothes" as the girls called them. I wanted clothes from Macy's like all the others. My parents stopped sewing for me. I assimilated.

By high school, I devoted much time, effort, and thought to my wardrobe, and the way I looked was very important to me and my parents. I devoured magazines, such as *Vogue* and *Glamour*, and emulated the looks I found there. The miniskirt revolution led by Twiggy and Mary Quant was in full swing and I was their poster child. My mother and I shopped every season in the department stores in Manhattan and in a local boutique called "Miss America." For my Sweet Sixteen, which we celebrated in a Chinese restaurant in Manhattan, I wore a fancy Swiss-dot cocktail dress. The proprietors of the restaurant surprised me with a traditional red Chinese embroidered coat and matching hat, which they lent me to wear for the night. Little did I know that forty years later, I would be collecting these very coats. In my senior year, when I began to work after school and earn some money, my parents still paid for everything. The money I made was to go for extra clothes. I was given free rein to buy and wear what I wanted and I chose my garments carefully to suit the sophisticated image I wanted to impart. I tore out photos from magazines, and brought these with me on my shopping trips with my mother. What we couldn't find or couldn't afford, my mother would sew for me, with me choosing the fabric that she would transform into exact replicas. I could show her the cover of *Vogue* on Friday afternoon, and by Sunday evening she would be pinning the garment on me for my first fitting. By Wednesday morning, I would be wearing the outfit to school.

Although they never did achieve the American dream, you never would have known it from looking at me. I dressed like a Jewish princess and was dubbed "the best in the Hall" when I graduated with honors from Erasmus Hall High School.

(left)
Youssef, the photographer, who was assigned to show me around Cairo, told me we were going to the holiest mosque in Cairo, so I dressed in my fantasy of what one should wear to such a holy site. The lattice work on my bag from the 1800s matches the lattice iron work on the arches. That's holy.

(below)
This was taken at the little kiosk in Tel Aviv across the street from where I was staying. I caused quite a stir that morning.

Tziporah Salamon

I wore pleated skirts and sweaters and shoes that I found in Greenwich Village on 8th Street at a store called Fred Braun. I was one of the cool ones, sophisticated and mature beyond my years. Although it was unspoken, I knew that it was up to me to achieve my mother's dream of living on Long Island, in a house with two cars, like all the other Jews who had made it. How was I going to do that? By marrying rich, by marrying up, by marrying the Prince. When it came time to apply to college, I applied to three schools: the University of Buffalo, my safe school, the University of Rochester, and the University of Pennsylvania, where I had the best chance of finding my prince. For my interview at the latter, my mother accompanied me on the long train ride from Brooklyn. On the way home, she informed me that she would take on an additional job, she would work even twenty-four hours if need be, to pay for the high tuition. Having seen the type of boys who were interviewing, she was determined that I go there, determined that her daughter, her "Mamashenele" would have entrance to the world of the rich and privileged and well-schooled. When the letters of rejection came in the mail, she cried, then said, "That's okay, Mamale, you'll go to Buffalo, your safe school."

Even though I was going to a state university, she still harbored the hopes that I would meet my prince, so she sent me away with a wardrobe fit for a princess. She made all of it: capes and culottes of beautiful tweeds and blouses of luscious silk, so that I was truly one of the best-dressed coeds on campus, very Ali MacGraw of *Love Story*. Alas, this look was short-lived as it was 1968, Kent State had just happened, and the University of Buffalo was considered "the Berkeley of the East." We took over the administration building, held rallies and marches, and came to blows with the National Guard. Girls were encouraged to burn their bras and don dungarees. When I showed up in my capes and culottes and high boots, I got teased. So I caved in: low-rise bell-bottom jeans and a purple leotard became my signature look and my mother's beautiful wardrobe sat in the closet.

I decided to do my junior year abroad, and applied to the University of Jerusalem. To transport a year's worth of clothes, we had a special trunk made and, once again, my mother got busy sewing, preparing my clothes. I was placed in an intermediate-level Ulpan to relearn my Hebrew and spent a glorious summer by the Sea of Galilee, studying during the week and exploring the country on the back of the 350 Honda of my American boyfriend on the weekends. However, I grew sadder and sadder as I realized that what I loved about Israel no longer existed. Instead of low-rise buildings and expansive skies, there were skyscrapers and highways; instead of dancing in the streets to Hebrew music, they were dancing in discotheques to Tom Jones; instead of drinking fresh-squeezed orange and grapefruit juice from the local kiosk, they were drinking Coca-Cola; instead of shopping in the local grocery stores, they were shopping in huge supermarkets. Everything I hated about America was now in Israel. I felt like America had done it to me twice—broken my heart. The old wound was reopened as I realized that I had no home. "You are not Israeli," they kept saying to me, "You are American." "You are Lynn, not Tzippy." My identity was shaken to the core and I cried

Wearing vintage Chinese minority pants found at a flea market, an antique beaded vest made from the top of an Afghanistan dress, a vintage Chinese minority belt, and an antique Bai woman's hat from the early 1900s worn over a beaded 1920s skull cap. One hat without the other doesn't work. I had them both for years and didn't wear either of them until one day I thought to combine them and voilà, magic!

until there were no tears left. To soothe my pain, I turned to food and quickly gained thirty pounds. No longer could I fit into my clothes. Instead, I donned dungarees and army fatigues and embroidered Bedoin dresses that I found in the Arab markets. I stopped going to visit my relatives, embarrassed to be seen with my new fat body. I denied myself the pleasure of both my loves; my family and my clothes. I ate some more. It was a battle I was to know for the next few decades of my life.

I returned to Buffalo and finished my senior year, graduating Phi Betta Kappa and Summa cum Laude with a degree in English literature and a certificate to teach secondary-school English. After college, I went out west to visit a friend in Berkeley, California, where it was love at first sight. I decided to make California my home and applied to graduate school at the University of California at Santa Barbara, taken by its beauty. After ensuring my acceptance, I set about traveling wherever the winds brought me. I ended up at the Gestalt Institute of Canada in Vancouver, British Columbia, where I was to live for three months.

My first night there, in our group meeting, Brian, the group leader, turned to me and said, "Lynn, tell us your story." I told them of my childhood in Israel, my move to America, and my name change. When they heard "Tziporah" they asked to call me that and thus my name was reborn. It was great for Gestalt work as "Tzippy" and "Lynn" had many conversations and I slowly learned to integrate the two.

When I returned to the English Department at UC Santa Barbara, I quickly switched to their education program, which had been started by a Gestalt therapist. My love affair with psychology and the human potential movement was in full bloom—as was my weight, which continued to rise. I now wore hippie clothes—full skirts with an elastic waistband, embroidered blouses, Mexican *huipils*, Indian dresses, wedge sandals, big earrings, and colorful head scarfs.

In spite of my girth, I still dressed—not in the beautiful fitted clothes of my teens, but in ethnic, hand-crafted attire that reflected the arty woman I was becoming. After graduating with a Master's Degree in Education, I relocated to Berkeley and became a teacher at Berkeley High School while pursuing a PhD in psychology at the California Graduate School of Family and Marital Therapy in San Rafael. My students would tell me that the only reason they came to class was to see what I was wearing. I was, indeed, a sight to behold, a poster girl for the flower children of San Francisco.

But by my second year of studies, working as a therapist in the field, I started to question my career choice. I loved the intimacy and ties that I found with my clients, but I could barely keep an emotional distance, often allowing our sessions to go on for hours for fear of cutting them off after the allotted hour while they were crying and pouring their hearts out. I had a hard time separating myself and setting boundaries and a voice in my head kept saying, "I have to have more fun. I can't listen to all this pain." I was reminded of the endless hours I had spent by my mother's side as I watched her suffer from migraines and listened to her painful memories, which she would recount to me in whispered tones, of the war, the loss of her family, the loss of her home, the loss of her

I had this Victorian lace capelet for years and nothing to wear with it until one day I found this fabulous skirt by a contemporary Israeli designer named Priscilla Gatica with the same cording effect it had. I love it when it comes together!

Tziporah Salamon

youth. I realized being a therapist was the role I took on in my family and I did not wish to take it on as a career.

To the chagrin of my parents, especially my father, I decided to quit my doctorate studies. "What am I going to tell my clients?" my father cried. "I've been telling them you're a doctor." "You just keep on telling them," I answered flippantly. "They'll never know the difference." But I, too, was somewhat shaken, as I no longer knew what I wanted to be. It was somewhat of a mid-life crisis when at the age of twenty-eight, I, who always had goals and ambition, found myself on shaky ground.

I decided to witness my life, to pay attention to what it was that I did. And I discovered myself going into the local boutiques on a regular basis, checking out the clothes, feasting my eyes on the merchandise, running my hands on the various clothes. A lightbulb went on in my head: "Ah, clothes. Of course. I always loved clothes." So I decided to change careers, move back to New York and pursue fashion. The week before I was scheduled to fly home, my father called and said, "Get on the next plane. Mom has cancer." So I moved back quickly. We began the search for her cure by going to all the cancer specialists on Park Avenue. One doctor promised to heal her by taking out her stomach, where the cancer lay, while telling me privately that her case was hopeless. So I took her to Boston to see a macrobiotic healer who introduced her to alternative treatments working with her diet. To my great relief, my mother opted for this latter treatment. I was able to begin my foray into the business of fashion.

With my love of theater, I thought costume design was a logical choice so I volunteered at Brooklyn College's theater department. They told me I needed to know how to sew. Now you would think, as a daughter of a seamstress mother and tailor father, I would naturally know how to sew, but no, I didn't, and I still don't. I had never expressed an interest, nor did my parents ever teach me. "You go read," my parents had told me, "so that your life will be easier." I signed up for a sewing course at Parsons. But in my first class, after countless attempts to thread the machine, I ended up bursting into tears, kicking the machine, and running out of the room, never to return. The pressure to "measure up" to my parents' expertise was too great and I failed miserably.

My first job in New York was at Victoria Falls, a beautiful boutique in SoHo that sold antique clothes. This was my introduction to Victorian whites and Victorian jet; Edwardian linen suits; '20s beaded dresses; '40s Joan Crawford suits; Chinese embroidered coats; and Chinese embroidered piano shawls. It was a jewel box of a store with sumptuous merchandise and I soaked in its beauty. The owner quickly realized my expertise with cloth and construction and assigned me as the buyer of fabrics and notions for the clothes she was reproducing downstairs in her workroom. My job was split between dealing with the high-end customers upstairs who bought our finery and the sewing department downstairs. It was quite an education. I even managed to sneak out a Victorian blouse one evening, taking it home for my mother to copy overnight and returning it the next day without the boss ever finding out. My mother was that good, that skilled and that determined to turn me into a lady. Unfortunately, she never managd to see the full transformation as she died in 1981, at

Vintage Chinese silk
pajamas whose buttons
I changed. I paid more
for the buttons than the
outfit. I love how the hat
totally echoes the red
buttons.

the age of sixty-two, the week I turned thirty-one. I was devastated, not knowing if I could survive without her as she and I were so symbiotic. It was as though my mother and I had made an unspoken pact: she would take care of me physically while I took care of her emotionally. She spent the last month of her life in the hospital, with me and my father and my sister going to visit every night. The night before she passed, we talked on the phone after I came back from the hospital and she told me, "I finished basting the garment. Now I can rest." These were her last words to me, as she then slipped into a coma from which she never recovered. The next day, April 11, 1981, a Saturday, I made my way to the hospital with difficulty, knowing this was the end. As my mother lay in her bed with tubes in her nose and eyes wide open staring at the ceiling, I climbed onto the bed beside her, holding her hand, and quietly singing to her all the Hebrew and Hungarian songs she sang to me as a little girl. Four days later, I turned thirty-one; my mother was thirty-one when I was born, also on a Saturday; 31 = 13 backward, the most important number in Jewish numerology, the numerical value of the word *Ahavah*, "love," in Hebrew.

My next job was at Charivari Men's Store, on the Upper West Side. Here I learned about men's clothes. I already knew about construction and fit—lessons that my father instilled in me at a tender age. But now I learned about the different designers: Armani; Cerruti; Zegna; Polo; Versace; Claude Montana. It was an invaluable lesson and I learned much, including the fact that I did not want to have my own shop. Although it did affirm my growing realization that my taste was right on as I noticed that invariably

the items that I loved the most were the ones chosen to be put in the window or on display on the mannequins in the shop.

Next I thought I would try being a buyer, so off I went to Barneys, working in the women's annex for seven dollars per hour with my poor dad lamenting, "For this I sent you to PhD school, so you could be a salesgirl?" But I persisted and again it was a great education. I would watch the elevator doors open and the most fashionable women in the world get off to shop. I learned the women's designers: Armani; Sonia Rykiel; Ralph Lauren; Missoni; Jean Paul Gaultier; and the Japanese: Issey Miyaki; Yohji Yamamoto; Matsuda; and my favorite, Comme des Garçons. In fact, I was the only one who really understood these Japanese designers, with their radical shapes, and deconstructed garments, so they gave me the Comme des Garçons boutique, where I managed to be the top salesgirl on the floor. As far as being a buyer, I watched closely to see if that was the job I wanted and I quickly realized that it wasn't. Sure, the buyers got to go off to Europe twice a year to see the collections, but most of the time they were holed up in a small cubicle dealing with price points and markdowns and paperwork and, no, this was not the job for me.

What about being a designer? I thought, surely this would be the right fit. Toward that end, I got a job at Norma Kamali, but I had to start on the floor in sales, with my poor father lamenting, "Still a salesgirl?" And I watched and saw Norma's daily work life which consisted of phone calls from Milan telling her they could no longer get that particular fabric or the dye lot had run out and other such calamities. This was far different from what I had envisioned; a whole different ball game from showing my mother the cover of *Vogue*, choosing the fabric, and having her make it up. No, I did not want to design on a mass level. This was not for me. Time to move on.

So I tried styling, getting a job with a stylist, where I would go to Bloomingdale's to either buy or return men's jockey shorts and women's housecoats to use in the beer or laundry detergent commercials we worked on. What does this have to do with my love of textiles, and fabric and beautiful design? I cried. Working for the advertising world was everything I was against: pushing on women products that they did not need; making them feel less than if they did not meet a certain criteria. The whole fashion world was rigged with elements that did not sit well with me. By 1981, even the shows, which were exciting the first year, had begun to seem mediocre after four years in the business. When the clothes were exciting and creative, they cost a fortune and were unattainable for most working women. I quickly became disillusioned and left the field.

Not sure what direction to go in next, I decided to follow the footsteps of all the creative women I knew who were pursuing their art while working in restaurants. I got a job as a waitress at a restaurant called Jezebel, owned by Alberta Wright, a brilliant woman who had owned an antiques store by the same name, known for its superior merchandise and frequented by stars such as John Lennon and Yoko Ono. The restaurant, located on the outskirts of the theater district, was decked out with the same beautiful textiles and clothing that she sold in the store. The seventeen tables were covered with antique piano shawls, beaded

dresses hung off the rafters, and beaded purses hung on the beaded lampshades of the antique lamps strewn around the dining room. A white lawn swing doubled for a bench and linen napkins and lace doilies lay on the tables where antique vases sat filled with beautiful flowers. The door to the women's bathroom was covered with an antique Japanese kimono, while the men's bathroom door was covered with a man's turn-of-the-century morning suit. It was like walking into your southern grandmother's attic, if your grandmother happened to have great taste.

The best part was that the waitresses—all of us Jezebels—were required to wear our own antique clothes. By this point I was wearing vintage clothes regularly, having realized that they were better made, one-of-a-kind, and cheaper than the designer clothes I coveted. For the first time, I had a boss who really stretched me. Alberta would bring me a different hat to wear each night and she herself was decked out to the nines. I paid close attention and learned and copied shamelessly. My style was taking off and I was beginning to turn heads. One day while I was working, a woman came up to me and introduced herself: "I am Wendy Goodman, fashion editor of *New York Magazine* and I want to do a shoot with you."

Sure enough, the following week she sent the most sought-after photographer in New York at the time, Cheryl Koralik, to my apartment and I grabbed three outfits out of my closet and we sneaked into the Ansonia—a beautiful prewar building on the Upper West Side—where Cheryl shot me on the window sill and on the stairs. There were no assistants, no crew, no makeup

artists, no stylists, no lights, not even a mirror—I changed outfits on the staircase. We did beautiful work together and even though the project never made it to press, I got the first photographs for my portfolio.

I loved my job and I was meeting fascinating people—movie stars and rock stars and Broadway royalty and famous screenwriters and actors, and every night was a scene and I was making more money than I ever had.... BUT. I knew I was cut out for more. One night I was lamenting to my friend Melissa, telling her of my frustrations and not knowing what I was meant to do with my gifts, and she suggested that I ask the question to God that night before falling asleep. I figured I had nothing to lose, so I did. And I had the following dream: The phone rang and my roommate answered it and gave it to me, "It's for you. It's Glenn Close." I got on the phone and said, "Hello, Ms. Close, I've always admired your work." "Tziporah, I hear you are a fashion consultant, I hear you are the best in the business. I want to hire you." I woke up, amazed by the dream, and called Melissa, who suggested I take my portfolio straight to Broadway where Glenn was appearing in a Broadway show called *The Benefactors*. I waited until Wednesday afternoon and went to the theater right after the matinee, asking at the ticket booth how I could see Ms. Close. They told me to knock on the red door. A big burly guy came out and when I told him I wanted to see Ms. Close, he naturally wanted to know if I had an appointment. When I said no, he refused to let me in. I was about to walk away, when, from behind him, came a woman who said to me, "Won't you come in? We've been waiting." What do you mean you've been waiting? I said to myself silently. Did you have the

same dream? I followed her down the maze, until we got to a door with a star on it, and out came Glenn Close herself saying, "Please come in. I've been waiting." At this point, I blurted out that I was not who they thought I was, but I assured her that if she just gave me five minutes of her time, I would explain everything. She invited me in and I told her of my dream and we started to talk about her relationship to clothes. I said to her, "Ms. Close, you have stardom written all over you. You will make it to the top with me or without me. With me in your life, you will just be a little bit more stylish as you get there." (This was 1984, before *Fatal Attraction* which catapulted her to the top.) She thanked me for my time and told me she had to think about it. Sure enough, a week later I received in the mail a beautiful, hand-written note saying how impressed she was with my moxie and flair but having thought about it she did not think she needed a stylist. Well, I thought, if God wants me to be this fashion consultant then let her do something about it.

In fact, I was a bit torn about this whole notion of dressing. You see, by now, I was heavily involved with Jewish Renewal, going to Temple on a regular basis and studying and attending Jewish retreats where I learned about the notion of Tikuun Olam, the repair of the world, which instructs that each of us is responsible to do her share to fix all that is broken in the world. Quite frankly, dressing seemed so superficial compared to big issues like global warming, poverty, illiteracy, world hunger. So I decided to forget about it and to go to Egypt, following an Egyptian friend who had gone back to live in Cairo. I was between jobs again and rather than getting another restaurant job,

My ode to Matisse, my master. When I spotted this robe in the flea market, my heart stopped. I had longed for it for years as I stared at Matisse's Purple Robe and Anemones in which the model is wearing such a coat, a replica of which was hanging on my wall for forty years.

Cairo seemed alluring and fresh with open-ended possibilities.

Living in Cairo was magical. I felt like I had stepped back in time, in some places as far back as Biblical days. Sometimes the earth I walked on seemed to be the same earth where Moses stepped. The streets were teeming with thousands of people, the cars and buses speeding by, sometimes coming to a halt as a herd of cows passed the highway. It was a Fellini movie come alive. I ended up teaching English at the British International School of Cairo where my students were the grandchildren of Presidents Nasser and Sadat, children of heads of major international companies and the daughters of a Saudi prince. A curious thing that happened to me on a regular basis was that almost every day, an older gentleman or a young boy would approach me, hand me a flower, and sing my praises. Although the entire speech was in Arabic, which I could hardly speak, I knew enough to know that they were appreciating and admiring my attire. In spite of the dire poverty and harsh living conditions, Egyptians knew and loved beauty and were generous with their praise and adoration. I was seen there in a way that I was not seen back home.

When I returned to New York, I got a job as a coat check at a hot new restaurant. Since I always dressed for the occasion, I decided that as a hat check girl I needed to wear hats. Thus started my serious hat collection, donning a different hat every day. I would build my whole outfit around the hat. It was a great creative exercise for me and I became a better dresser. The customers were so delighted with my attire that they kept increasing their tips, so that I could now really shop. And

shop I did. I was the first on line at every vintage show and there were several a year. I loved Victorian and Edwardian clothes and I easily spotted the best finds. I also loved ethnic and anything hand-embroidered, and I started amassing some rare beauties. The vendors began to recognize me and knew what I loved and would bring in special items for me. They also knew that I would do justice to their pieces, creating a whole ensemble that was a work of art, so they were willing to work with me, holding things if necessary until I could pay them off. It helped that I was now featured regularly in Bill Cunningham's style sections in The *New York Times*. I would see Bill on an almost regular basis as he typically stood on 5th Avenue and 57th Street and I would pass him on my way to visit my father who, having retired from his own tailoring business at the age of seventy-seven, was back at work at the Bergdorf Goodman women's alterations department. Bill would see me and break out in a big grin, smiling appreciatively at my outfit. I would stop to say hello and we would chat for a few minutes. Often, we looked at the Bergdorf windows together, admiring their creativity and critiquing the designs. He was a fan from the start and even sent me love letters thanking me for "soaring his spirits."

My inner transformation, the shift that turned everything around for me, happened very unexpectedly. It was during the summer of 1999 when I was working at a Jewish spiritual retreat called Elat Chayyim in Woodstock, New York. The first Shabbat, Rabbi Shefa Gold asked if there was anyone who wanted to dress the Torah. I never heard of dressing the Torah, but I loved the idea so I naturally raised my hand. When I walked up

I love stripes any way I can get them. Here I pair a Victorian vest with a Dries Van Noten skirt and vintage hat. Nothing beats black and white.

to the front where the Torah lay on the table, she smiled and said, "Yes, I noticed you were a good dresser." With that acknowledgment, everything shifted. The waters had parted, I had crossed over. Somehow, all the angst and turmoil I had felt, all the doubts and misgivings I had about dressing, just melted. I had received the rabbi's blessings and it was good. It was holy. My dressing was good. My dressing was holy.

Later on in the summer, Reb Zalman Schachter-Shalomi, the granddaddy of Jewish Renewal came up to celebrate his seventy-fifth birthday. Upon seeing me for the first time he said, "You represent Hod on the tree of life." In Kabbalah, Hod, one of the attributes to which Jews aspire, stands for splendor and humility. Again, my dressing was found favorable in the eyes of the rebbe. What a great honor. What a great relief. Every week guests would come up to me to thank me and tell me that they looked forward to my entering a room because when I did so I elevated the energy. Could it be? Was my dressing a holy act? Did God actually want me to be this dresser? Was this my Tikuun Olam, my way of bettering the world? I wept as I heard a resounding "YES"! I had found the reason for my being at last. From that summer on, I owned my talent, I allowed myself to dress and to dress as well as I could. I picked up the baton and ran with it. There was no holding me back.

In the fall of 2000, on the Jewish holiday Simchat Torah, while we were dancing with the scrolls on West End Avenue, I met a woman by the name of Lucie Porges. Lucie, a Holocaust survivor from Vienna, was a gifted and successful fashion designer who had worked alongside Pauline Trigere and

now was teaching a course at Parsons School of Continuing Education called Design Atelier. She happened to live across the street from me and we had started seeing each other on the street as she was waiting for the bus and I was zooming by on my bicycle. "Look at you. Look at the way you dress. You're a work of art. Come teach my class," she implored me one day. "What am I going to teach them? I am an English teacher," I blurted out. "Bring your clothes. Just show them your outfits," she said. And that's what I did. Twice a year, on the final week of the course when the students were over at her apartment for wine and cheese and final evaluation, I would pack up my outfits and walk across the street to Lucie's apartment where I would lay out the clothes, the hats, the shoes, the bags, the sunglasses, the gloves and tell my story. That was the start of my course, *The Art of Dressing*.

By 2005, I had taught the class ten times, each time showing different outfits, and the class was beginning to morph into a one-woman show in my head. I signed up for a Master Storyteller workshop with Peninnah Schram, a renowned storyteller, at the 92nd Street Y. "You have five minutes to think of a ten-minute story to tell the class," she informed us. The beginning of my story wrote itself: papa was a tailor; mama was a dressmaker; I was born in Israel.... I came home, and the rest of the story came tumbling out of me. *The Fabric of My Life*, my one-woman show, a sartorial autobiography, had been birthed. The pieces of the puzzle, the threads of my life, were finally being woven into a complete tapestry; and it was good.

I can never have enough antique Chinese clothes. The luscious silk and exquisite embroidery send me over the moon.

(following spread)
I love how the swirls in the sleeves of the contemporary sweater echo the swirls of the Victorian cape and the ruffles in the Victorian scarf.

Tziporah Salamon

STYLE ESSENTIALS

Imagine, dear reader, opening up your closets and delighting in its contents. Imagine loving everything in your wardrobe. Imagine looking forward to the seasons changing so you can put on that sweater and wool skirt from last winter, or the linen pants and cotton blouse from three summers ago. Imagine leaping out of bed so you can create a work of art that you assemble on your body with items of clothing that not only protect you from the elements, but express who you are, your heritage, your vision, that put a bounce in your step, a flutter in your heart, and a smile on the face of all who see you. All this is possible if you dress well and follow a few simple steps.

First and Foremost, Know Your Body

Take an honest stock of what looks good on you. Go to a department store and try on different shapes, different patterns, different colors. Experiment. Choose a bottom. Do you look better in pants, or a skirt, or is a dress the most suitable for your body. What shape? Cigarette-shape pants or a wide leg? High-waisted, or below the waist? Whatever the shape you settle on, remember that the length of the pants should end at the ankle bone, not below the shoe. This is a mistake that so many women make and one that really makes a difference. Pants that end at the ankle bone look chicer. They also allow you to see the shoes and socks, which add another dimension and element of interest to the overall effect.

Invest in Staples

When first building a wardrobe, choose
a dark color that will go with most things.
Black is the obvious choice but navy blue
or grey is just as good. Invest in staples.
A crisp white blouse. A black turtleneck
sweater. A well-fitted and well-made jacket.
A good pair of shoes. A great bag. When
I was first starting out in the fashion
field in my early 30s the above staples
were all I owned. I varied these with my
accessories—jewelry, scarves, hats.

Buy the Best That Your Budget Will Allow
Quality Over Quantity.

Better to have one great well-made garment that will last a lifetime than five inferior ones that will disintegrate and fall apart after a few seasons.

Timeless and Classic Rather Than Trendy and Of-The-Moment

Choose pieces that will not date, that will stand up to the test of time, and that will serve you for decades. Remember, fashion is of the moment; style is forever. Fashion is fickle and changes every season—it is the only way a multi-billion-dollar industry stays alive. Style endures and gives you character. Style sets you apart from others. Style is yours and yours alone.

Accessorize! Accessorize! Accessorize!

This is where the fun starts. Be creative with your jewelry: mix high and low, real gold and fake, real pearls and costume. Load up your arms with bangles, add a necklace or two or three, and always wear earrings as they frame the face. Change sunglasses, add a scarf, wear a hat, pin a flower to your lapel, or place a rose behind your ear. Change the buttons. I always use antique buttons that I find in flea markets rather than the plastic ones found on most new garments. In the old days, buttons were made of real stones—they were akin to jewelry and made the garb look so much richer. Buttons are an easy way of transforming a favorite old piece and giving it new life: instant pop.

Good Shoes and a Good Handbag Are A Must

This is worth the investment. Protect your leather goods by taking good care of them—with regular polishing and repairs at the shoemaker. Shoes are expensive so consider buying them on sale. Buy shoes that fit and that you can walk in comfortably. There is nothing more painful than an ill-fitting shoe. I cannot wear high heels and am most comfortable in a kitten heel or wedge. I also love mules, which I find so feminine and which force me to pay attention to my posture and carriage—an added bonus. I love the sound they make as I come down the stairs, utterly charming.

Enlist the Services of a Good Seamstress and Tailor

Men know the importance of well-fitted garments. They regularly have their clothes altered to suit their bodies, and this is a must for any well-dressed woman as well. I employ at least three dressmakers at a time to alter and repair my clothes which, because they are mainly antique, readily fall apart as the thread unravels or seams open up. I also often have favorite pieces copied. I have had my original Armani knickers that I bought in 1982 copied in various fabrics and colors, as they are my favorite shape and I have never again found a pair of pants that I like as much. In the long run, this will save you money and it will also give work to craftsmen.

Consider the Whole Effect; You Are Creating a Work of Art, a Painting

Every element in the ensemble has to work with the other elements; they all have to tell the same story. This is one of the principles of design—harmony. Both our eye and our mind crave this. When I am assembling an outfit, I think of the total look. If I am going for an Asian look, every piece in the ensemble has to look Asian, including the accessories. When I am going for a Pierrot look, every piece has to add to the overall effect of looking like a clown. A big collar, a ruff, pom-poms, diamond shapes: the whole is only as good as the sum of its parts. Think of it as storytelling, with every element of the outfit enhancing the story. Nautical? Striped top and wide-legged pants. Romantic? High-collared lace blouse and full skirt. Arty? Bold stripes with statement jewelry and over-size glasses. Dressing is an artistic endeavor with you as the painter, your body as your canvas, the various components of your outfit as the paints, and your eyes as your brush.

Consider Adding Color

Many women are afraid of color and shy away, but it's actually a great way to spruce up your wardrobe. Start by choosing a favorite color and adding it to your black or white basics. Combine a pair of black pants with a red sweater, add red shoes and red lipstick, and voila, a work of art. Or team a blue blouse and a white skirt, add a blue flower to your hair and blue sunglasses, and you are good to go. I like to repeat the color in bundles of three; this way there is uniformity and some sort of order and method to your scheme. Once comfortable with color, go with it. Although I wear mostly black in the winter, I love wearing color in the summer. Coral should be in every woman's summer wardrobe. Also lemonade yellow, which is so refreshing; green, reminiscent of grass and nature; blue, reminding us of the sky and sea. There is no color I don't wear and I, for one, do not adhere to the "Color Me Beautiful" theory of color. I love them all and wear them all.

Pattern

I love stripes and polka dots. There is nothing more appropriate for summer than a blue and white striped T-shirt à la Picasso and Chanel. Classic and chic, it is an instant and easy way of looking cool. The same with polka dots, especially classic blue and white. I own two polka-dot dresses and a pair of polka-dot pants that I pair with a polka-dot blouse and capelet, and a polka-dot hat. All the polka dots are different sizes, which adds to the charm, so that the four garments look whimsical together, eliciting comments and smiles wherever I go. The winning combination of black and white is always chic and never gets old. There is no better color combination and no better way to stand out in a crowd. Worn in any format: black pants, white blouse, black ballet flats, and red lipstick—there is no better look for summer. Or white pants, black top, white sandals, black straw hat, black sunglasses—instant chic. A great travel tool is to pack only black and white, keeping it simple and yet keeping the bar high.

Texture Is Another Element to Consider

The different materials in the outfit have to work with one another. Silk goes best with silk; cotton goes with cotton, denim, or linen; wool goes with wool, cashmere, or silk. Fabrics also need to be able to endure the activity they are called upon to do. Silk is too delicate for playing tennis or working out, just as velvet is too fine to wear to the office but splendid for holiday entertaining. The same with shoes—a strappy sandal looks best with a summer dress, while sturdy oxfords, brogues, loafers, or a pump work with a wool suit. Long dangling earrings look great with a gown or dress, while classic clip-ons are more suited for sporty attire.

We Come Now to an Important Element of Design—Balance

There are two ways to achieve this in dress: one is through perfect symmetry—imagine a line going down your body with each side being the mirror image of the other. Perfect symmetry is achieved by straight lines that impart force and formality and command authority. A well-fitted suit is a perfect example of this.

The second way to achieve this is through informal balance, which can happen by, say, counterbalancing a gathering on the right shoulder with a gathering on the left hip, forcing your eye to go from one to the other and yet achieving a perfect balance. Think of a gown cut on the bias with a pin on the right shoulder and a flower behind your left ear. Chic, elegant, and perfectly appealing to the eye.

The Last Important Element of Design
Is Proportion

This requires a woman to take into consideration her height and build when assembling an outfit. Tall, thin women can carry a large handbag and look great in oversize clothing that would totally overwhelm a short woman with a small frame. This is where the mirror is your best ally, as is a good seamstress. A boxy top can work wonders on a short woman and hides a multiple of sins. Longer lines are more suited for a tall frame. However, there are no absolutes here and your best bet is trial and error. I work with my seamstresses and have them pin up the hem of a dress or jacket until we arrive at the perfect scale. I must confess, I have been known to have the seamstress redo the finished garment, once I determined that the proportion is still not right. This used to drive my father crazy, while my mother, a bit more lenient and tolerant of my perfectionism, totally understood.

Consider Dressing for the Occassion

Where are you going? Obviously going to work calls for one kind of outfit while going to the opera calls for another. I dress casually to run my errands; artistically and colorfully to go to a museum; and festively to go to a party. Of course, my idea of "casual" may not be yours, but part of the fun of dressing is taking into account where you are headed, who you will be with and who will see you, and what you will be doing. Plan accordingly. No matter what, always dress as well as you can, and in a becoming and thought-out outfit. Dress well so that you can look down at your body and it will give you joy. Dress well so that you can have the confidence to take on whatever challenge life may throw you. In return, you are likely to get smiles and compliments from perfect strangers, to meet people you would not otherwise meet, perhaps even get invited to events and parties. Most importantly, you will feel good about yourself knowing that you are doing your small part in making this a more beautiful world.

ZIVA
NAUMANN

Ziva's generosity of spirit extends to her wardrobe—she is always adorned with interesting hand-crafted jewelry made by talented women artisans she loves to promote.

It's fitting that I start the interview with Ziva in her kitchen, as she is one of the best cooks I've ever known. Ziva Sirkis Naumann was born in Palestine to Polish parents. She was close to her grandfather, a wealthy textile factory owner in Poland, who, impassioned by the Zionist speeches of Theodore Herzl, moved his wife and ten children to Palestine to replenish the land. Ziva's father, a farmer, built orchards throughout Palestine.

Ziva's passions for beauty and fine handwork were ignited by her mother's beautiful embroidery. Her first spark of "fashion" was kindled by the Bedoin embroidered dresses worn by her mother's housekeeper, Omni. Thus started Ziva's lifelong affair with ethnic garbs with exquisite embroidery. It's these dresses that Ziva dons for the countless Shabbat dinners, Passover seders, Bar and Bat Mitzvahs of her large family that she presides over as matriarch and also head chef.

Ziva immigrated to the U.S. with her first husband and two sons in 1958, working at the Israeli consulate in New York. Ten years later, she moved to Los Angeles with her second husband and four sons and when that marriage fell apart supported her family through her successful catering company. She ended up working for The Family Law section of Legal Aid as an administrator. In 1981, when the Reagan administration cut the funds, leaving their 445 clients without prompt legal assistance, she took matters into her own hands, put an ad in UCLA's law school for volunteers, and, with Ethel Levitt, a volunteer attorney, opened an office called Levitt and Quinn. Their practice quickly grew and became a beacon of hope for poor women who ordinarily could not afford legal aid. Word of the dedication of "the grandmothers" spread and recognition followed, including a segment on *60 Minutes* entitled, "My grandmother, the lawyer." After eighteen years of service to Levitt and Quinn as the center's director, Ziva is semi-retired but continues to head up fund-raising efforts. Without her, Levitt and Quinn would not be the successful law firm that it is today, helping more than 250,000 clients. The Ziva building, which the firm is housed in, was dedicated in 2000 to honor her work as its founder and director.

Ziva's priority in life is helping others. Her innate style, natural beauty, and inborn elegance serve her in navigating life—but they are not her priority. She finds all her clothes in thrift stores and prides herself on thrifting in every country she visits. She spends no more than twenty dollars on any item and never reads fashion magazines. And yet, her wardrobe is extraordinary: hand-embroidered Palestinian robes; Mexican dresses; Bedouin dresses; hand-woven pants and jackets from Vietnam. She has a collection of caftans by a Mexican designer named Josefa, which once belonged to Loretta Young and that she bought at her local thrift store, tipped off by a loyal worker who called her when it first came in. At eighty-five she still stands erect, rocks a pair of heels, and often wears jeans. She is always adorned with interesting jewelry, usually made by talented artisans she loves to promote. Her generosity of spirit extends to her wardrobe as well—she wears and spreads the word about handcrafted items made by women all over the world, from Be'er Sheva to Haiti.

I claim Ziva as my kindred mother. What brought us together is our love of textiles. It was the summer of 2005, my father had just passed, and I was going back to Israel to

mourn him. An acquaintance gave me the name of a colleague who worked at Shenkar School of Design in Tel Aviv. Era Lev was the head of the archives division and she invited me to look through the collection. What jumped out at me were twelve pieces, each with a different design but all with the same exquisite handwork, the most beautiful colorful, intricate embroidery I had ever seen. "Hold everything," I blurted. "Where do I find pieces like this?" Era promptly assured me that all this was long gone, having been made by a young Yemenite woman who walked barefoot to Israel with the mass exodus of Jews from Yemen. Era, however, did know of another Yemenite woman, Mazal Cohen, a collector of these antique textiles, who might be willing to show me her collection. Two buses later, I was greeted at the front door by Mazal, a stunning Semitic beauty. As she welcomed me in, she commented that I looked just like her mother-in-law, Ziva Naumann.

A year later, back in New York, Ziva called to invite me to lunch. As I saw my reflection reflected back to me in the woman who greeted me, I could only pray and wish that I too would be this radiant, vibrant, and stunning in twenty years. As we got to know each other over lunch, I learned that her oldest son was born on April 15, 1950, my birthday. Ziva was giving birth to her son at the same time that my mother was giving birth to me. When I visited her in her home in Los Angeles I discovered that not only could I fit into everything in her closet, but, most importantly, I actually wanted to wear everything in her closet.

I am truly my "mother's" daughter, hoping to impact the world with even a fraction of her accomplishments—and always in style. Ziva is a role model for us all.

Ziva is a splash of color in this Mexican caftan, multicolored straw hat, and rings by Nayeli Alvarez.

This is a woman who
loves patterns, textures,
embroidery and color,
both in her dress and
her home décor.

An exquisite hand-
embroidered Palestinian
dress, reflecting Ziva's
heritage and extraordi-
nary taste.

BEATRIX

OST

"I am fierce because I am truthful.
I tell it like it is. You get what you see."

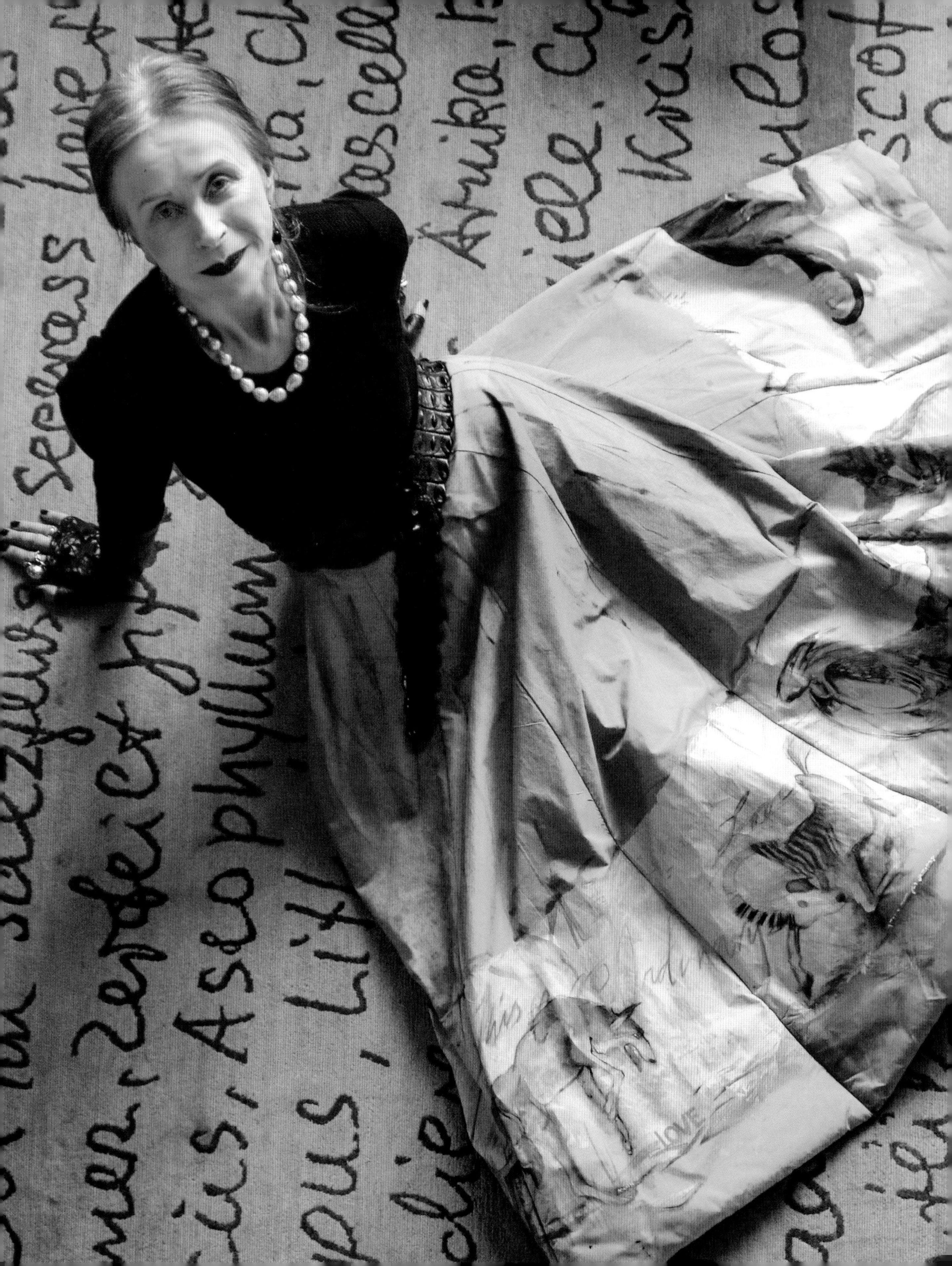
LOVE

We visit Beatrix in her duplex apartment in one of New York City's landmark buildings. She greets us with a warm smile and a pot of tea. "Come in," she beckons, as we enter the spacious living room with its huge windows and art all around, mostly done by Beatrix herself. An artist, sculptor, writer, actress, and producer, Beatrix was born in Stuttgart and in her youth studied at the Academy of Fine Arts in Munich and with the Expressionist artist Oskar Kokoschka.

She tells us that with International Women's Day coming up next week, someone asked her if she would be their "fierce woman," a title that sits well with Beatrix. "I am fierce because I am truthful," she says. "I tell it like it is. You get what you see." Whereas growing up, her sister was "the beauty," Beatrix was "the brain." She was the one who made her father, a pessimist, laugh, the one who was praised by him for being smart.

My Father's House, Beatrix's book about growing up in wartime Bavaria on a large estate, came about as a result of Beatrix finding a stack of love letters from her father to her mother during World War II. Her father, an officer in the army, was sent away to Africa to be City and Harbor Commander of Tubruq, Libya, where he befriended the local merchants and purchased their fabulous wares, which he sent back home to Germany. While there, he also became friends with Field Marshal Erwin Rommel, one day telling him that the war was lost, a treasonable offense. Rommel could have easily had him executed but instead sent him home to "feed Germany," citing a likely nervous

breakdown. So Beatrix survived the war on their farm with "all that really mattered," both parents and food and shelter.

This, too, is when she experienced her first shock of style. At the age of five, she took her father's tie and tied it around her tiny waist to make the dress her mother put on her conform to her body and her taste. When her two aunts came to visit, dressed in American officer army jackets, flowers in their lapels, wearing platform heels and rakish hats, little Beatrix knew this was who she was going to be.

While she easily could have become a designer, she chose to become a painter because she knew the commercial side of fashion would totally bore her. The whole notion of what's in and what's out and fashion's quick turnover does not interest her. Yet she is considered a great style icon. The designers, Mary-Kate and Ashley Olsen, named her as the inspiration for their Fall 2010 collection, and she continues to inspire a new generation of designers and stylists. She is currently involved in a project called Article 22, for which she is designing jewelry and teapots to be handmade in Laos out of land mines and unexploded bombs found after the war.

When I ask her about her sense of style, and what it takes to achieve it, she asserts that first and foremost is her sense of self. She insists that she is not a shopper but rather a collector, and that she keeps her clothes for years, augmenting them with the occasional newly acquired piece. Many of her garments, including her shoes and thigh-high boots, are bespoke and she often designs them herself.

Beatrix favors a late Edwardian style,

126

peplum jackets over narrow skirts, hats
and turbans and ankle boots worn alongside
pieces from such avant-garde designers
as Comme des Garçons, Junya Watanabe,
Yohji Yamamoto, and Azzedine Alaïa. On
this particular morning she is wearing
a lime green skirt by Ronaldus Shamask,
hand-painted with animals by the artist
John Owen, who also painted the floors to
the entrance of the apartment. She pairs it
with a black undershirt from La Perla, an
Ann Demeulemeester crocodile belt, and
custom-made boots. On her fingers are her
signature rings; two are her own designs of
twigs that wrap around her fingers up to
her first knuckles, tributes to the landscape
where she lives on a farm in Charlottesville,
Virginia. The other two are from Venice; one
features a large pearl entwined by a snake;
the other a memento mori skull. On her pinky
is a ring of her own design made of bomb
materiel. In her ears are lovely hanging onyx
from the thirties and in her signature blue
hair she wears a turban of Fortuny-like silk.

The overall effect is one of utter femininity and timeless glamour. I tell her that
she reminds me of a modern-day Anaïs Nin.
Like Anaïs, delicate and fine-boned with
an old-world charm and arresting beauty,
Beatrix owns her sexuality and is not afraid
of her femininity. Her whole being—from
her laughter, her writings, her outfits, her
artwork, her surroundings, her homes,
and the food she serves—exude a sensuality,
a knowing, an unabashed sense of self.
Beatrix Ost is one fierce woman indeed!

A form-hugging dress
by Alexander McQueen,
emphasizing Beatrix's
delicate and shapely figure.

(opposite)
Prowling the city as an
urban warrior, Beatrix
is a vision to behold.

132

AMY
FINE
COLLINS

Amy is one of the last hold outs of an age
when women dressed, when one took the
time to learn from the masters by studying
the great paintings.

Amy Fine Collins, a writer at *Vanity Fair*, where she writes about art, fashion, and design, has been a fixture on the New York City fashion scene for decades. Not only is she on the International Best Dressed List "Hall of Fame," she sits on the prestigious committee of four that selects the men and women who make the cut. Seen often at New York's chicest parties and always dressed to the nines, Amy sets the bar high indeed.

Born in Fairfield, Connecticut, and raised in Bucks County, Pennsylvania and Knoxville, Tennessee, to a mother who was an artist and art historian and a father who was a psychoanalyst and a clotheshorse, Amy grew up in a household that valued good clothing and being well-dressed. With frequent visits to museums and dance performances, young Amy inherited not only her mother's artistic ability and eye, but also her rigorous aesthetic standards. For the impressionable young girl, who often sat for her mother as a model, every detail of her mother's clothing left an indelible mark. Her own childhood wardrobe, such as the fine Liberty of London lawn dresses that her mother painstakingly sought out for her daughters, sparked in Amy a love of all things beautiful and well made.

Amy studied art history, earning degrees from Swarthmore College and Columbia University, where she also taught. She eventually landed at *Vanity Fair*, her perfect home base. After writing a piece on Geoffrey Beene's twenty-fifth-anniversary retrospective at the National Academy of Design, the master designer invited her to lunch, wanting to know how she could know him better than he knew himself just by viewing his designs. That fateful meeting led to a sixteen-year friendship in which she served as Mr. Beene's

"amuse": "a" for Amy, his muse, who inspired and amused him. This important relationship helped Amy consolidate her visual identity and she found herself in his clothes.

It was during this period that Amy came to my attention. I remember the first time I saw a photograph of this thin, tall woman with striking cropped black hair and impeccable style. It was an arresting image that sparked my curiosity to learn more about her. When I happened to see her in person at Doyle Auction House at their now-defunct fabulous annual auction of clothes, textiles, and accessories, I secretly inched myself closer to get a better look. As I took in every detail of her outfit, the cut of her dress, the sharpness of her hair, the perfect Manolo Blahnik suede mules, she did not disappoint. She is a walking work of art.

Indeed, Amy's childhood years as an observer has enabled her to look at herself objectively, to see herself as an object, a painting. Her view of dressing is similar to mine: clothing and accessories are the paints that allow a woman to present herself as a living embodiment of art. Dressing is an artistic visual form of self-expression, one that brings both the dresser and the viewer immense satisfaction.

Part of the joy is discovering that this goes with that; i.e., how well a new purchase can work with an older item in your closet. To this day, Amy has a large portion of her Geoffrey Beene pieces, which she still wears. She also wears other designers who inspire her. Her rule of thumb is that she doesn't wear clothes by people she doesn't know. Her wardrobe today consists of pieces from Thom Browne; Lanvin by Alber Elbaz; Oscar de la Renta; Carolina Herrera; Azzadine Alaïa; Ralph

Rucci; Zac Posen; Isaac Mizrahi; Alice and Olivia—all of whom are personal friends. She also wears the clothing of new lesser-known designers to whom she serves as a mentor and muse, such as Angel Sanchez; Asher Levine; Norisol Ferrari. She wears Manolo Blahnik shoes exclusively.

Amy is fiercely loyal to the designers and friends whose creations allow her to uphold her high standards and singular vision. She favors garments with a strong graphic line and a bit of severity, as opposed to any fussy ornamentation. This visual preference is evidenced in her home decor as well. Her sprawling apartment on Park Avenue is filled with colorful graphic rugs, bold and dramatic sofas, portraits of Helena Rubenstein on the wall, and colorful striped curtains on the windows. Here lives a woman thoroughly informed by art history, whose trained eye has created the perfect backdrop for her striking sartorial choices.

Amy is one of the last holdouts of an age when women dressed; when fashion photographers looked to art not fashion photography, to inform their visions; when one took the time to learn from the masters by studying the great paintings. In an age where clothing has become disposable and mass-produced, Amy Fine Collins is indeed fashion royalty and leads by very fine example.

(previous spread)
Amy wears a dress by
Thom Browne, with
his signature red/white/
blue stripes etched in
the side slit.

(opposite)
This sleeveless dress
exposes Amy's arms,
finely chiseled from
years of swimming.

MICHELE

OKA

DONER

Michele keeps her sartorial choices simple, allowing her to devote her time and energy to her work. "In a way, this is my lab coat," she says of her signature column dress.

I enter the SoHo loft of artist Michele Oka Doner and am immediately transported to another world. On the walls are dozens of the anthropomorphic porcelain talismans, "soul catchers," that she has been making since 1984. On a table in the sitting area are a trio of fish, each swimming in individual "aquarium"s, actually etched-glass bowls set in crystal and cast-bronze coral-form cradles, created by Michele for her 2005 Reef collection commissioned by Steuben. Next to the kitchen is a labyrinthine library rich in volumes on art, archaeology, and the natural sciences.

There is much commotion going on in this sun-drenched live/work space as several assistants are crating Michele's work for her next exhibition, a retrospective of her work, spanning more than fifty years, "How I Caught a Swallow in Midair," to open at the Perez Museum in Miami, Florida. Michele is an internationally acclaimed artist and author, whose work can be found in many public collections including the American Museum of Natural History, the Metropolitan Museum of Art, the Art Institute of Chicago, the National Design Museum, and the Smithsonian Institute. Her work encompasses sculpture, public art, jewelry, and furniture.

Michele is perhaps best known for numerous public art commissions including *Radiant Site* at New York's Herald Square subway station and *A Walk on the Beach* at the Miami International Airport, which is composed of more than nine thousand bronzes embedded with mother-of-pearl in terrazzo, taking the form of marine life and seashells. Whether working in clay, bark, mud, wood, bronze, wax, paper, or glass, her works are infused with a lifelong study and appreciation of nature, often blurring the lines between artifacts and artworks. The portraits on the wall look in her loft like charcoal drawings, but upon closer inspection you see they are really twigs and tiny leaves; what looks like a real seashell is actually made of ceramics; the little chair of thrones, which seems to be made of branches, is really bronze. It is this ability to combine elements from the natural and man-made world and infuse them with her deep interest and knowledge of mythology and ancient societies that has informed her career.

Michele grew up in Miami, with its giant banyan trees and unpopulated beaches, and she remembers the pungent smell of the smoke from the nearby fires of the Everglades—all of which she channeled into her art. "For me, nature is a powerful thing, intoxicating and enchanting," she explains. "In the East, in Japan in particular, nothing in nature is taken for granted. In the West we have adopted a disposable approach to life, having largely lost our reverence for nature and our connection to the beauty that is around us. I suppose through my work I am trying to reestablish that."

The middle daughter of a mother with a high visual literacy and a father who was one of the first three Jews to get into Harvard, becoming a lawyer and judge and later the mayor of Miami, Michele sees herself as a professional woman with a feminine bent. She is proud of her matriarchal heritage, which goes back to an elegant grandmother from Romania. Her mother, a former Latin teacher, was a Jungian who understood the importance of clothes and how to dress and passed this skill along to her three daughters. Using the beautiful fabrics that she brought back from her travels to Egypt, India, and

Syria, she had her clothes made, along with matching dresses for her daughters.

On this day, Michele is wearing her signature column dress in white, reminiscent of the himation of ancient Greece. She first had this dress made for her in 1987 by a Chelsea designer and since then she's had them made up in various colors and fabrics, such as silk, cashmere and silk velvet. "In a way, this is my lab coat," she says. She prefers to keep her sartorial choices simple—allowing her to devote her time and energy to her work. One good black dress purchased yearly is really all she needs. She never wears jeans; they don't fit her well as her legs are longer in proportion to her torso. She wanted a different look and found it in simple dresses. She favors the dresses of Morgane Le Fay, a SoHo designer she has worn for years, as well as Comme des Garçons, Jean Paul Gaultier, and shoes by Robert Clergerie. She keeps herself busy and moving, honors her body as the temple that it is, and exudes good health, pride, and a fierce sense of self. She has no investment in staying the same and welcomes and embraces aging as the natural evolution that it is.

Michele has been an artist her whole life. She believes it is our primal power to manifest an idea, to materialize one's curiosity just as "a bird gets up and knows its song." She views her home as a laboratory of living and life as a ceremony and work of art. It's this seamless fusion between art and life that is her greatest accomplishment. It makes perfect sense that late on Friday afternoons Michele likes nothing more than to visit the Egyptian wing of the Metropolitan Museum of Art. Dressed in her simple Romanesque column, with her hair pulled back in a simple bun, Michele Oka Doner is our modern-day priestess.

(opposite)
A woman at work.
An artist in her element.

(above)
Michele in her signature
column dress in white
with a hard hat and pearls.

VALERIE

VON

SOBEL

Valerie's ensembles are always unique,
charming, and downright playful.
She is never "worn by her clothes";
rather, she puts her own spin on them.

Valerie Von Sobel first came to my attention when she was featured on the blog of photographer Ari Seth Cohen, creator of *Advanced Style*. Struck by her exquisite and refined taste and elegance, I was fascinated to learn more. I discovered that she is an accomplished actress, interior designer, and artist, as well as the founder of a charity, The Andre Sobel River of Life Foundation, named after her beloved son, who died of an inoperable brain tumor. The foundation provides emergency assistance within twenty-four hours to single caregivers of children suffering from catastrophic or life-threatening illnesses who are in financial crisis.

When I learned that Valerie is also a survivor of the Communist era, who fled her native Hungary during the 1956 uprising against the Soviet regime, it gave me the impetus to send off an email, introducing myself as a fellow Hungarian and suggesting that, as I happened to be visiting Los Angeles, we meet for strudel and tea. Coincidentally, a few hours later, while stopping for lunch at Barneys, we met not by design but by accident. I spotted her and happily approached the object of my admiration. Thus began a friendship in which we have since spent countless of hours discussing the elusive subject of style, a topic dear to both our hearts.

"It takes an interest and discernment," Valerie says. "It always starts with curiosity. You have to be devoted to the subject. It comes from a deep desire to express, whether it be a garden or architecture. If you understand proportion, texture, the mixing of unusual elements and adornments, all your aesthetic expressions will sing the same tune. It's both instinctual and developed. There is a hunger to express. You see a certain piece and you want to own it and you may be the only one to desire it. You see in your head what you will do with it. It comes together in your imagination and you have an urge to manifest it. You become an extension of the designer's intention and complete him by wearing it in your way."

Valerie's earliest memories of style were lifted from a few copies of *Vogue* she acquired at the tender age of nine or ten. In these pages her interest in clothes was honed and refined. Growing up in Communist Hungary, where you could shine only through standing out, her mother was impeccably groomed, wearing beautiful hats, and taking great care with her hair and makeup, all of which young Valerie "inhaled." Once or twice a year they would go to the corset maker where Valerie had her first custom bathing suit made.

In l956, when they left Hungary and arrived in Canada, a whole world opened up to the impressionable young girl. Who am I? How am I going to make a living? What will make me look good? Valerie's first forays into fashion were driven by the desire to fit in, to survive in this new world. A few years later when she was discovered and signed to 20th-Century Fox, the same desire to fit in, this time in Hollywood, was her primary objective. She quickly adapted and her innate intelligence and immense curiosity aided her in finding her way. When the studio collapsed, she became an interior decorator, mentored by some of the truly great ones. She spent years honing that craft, and along with it, fashion, in which she saw a great similarity. Valerie became less and less interested in trying to fit in and more and more confident in invention. She wore pieces by Paco Rabbane, Comme des Garçons, Yohji Yamamoto, and Gianfranco Ferre, whose

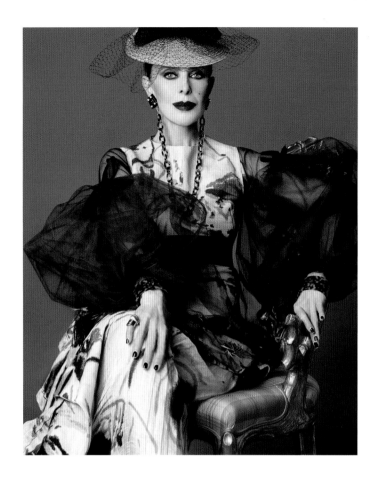

(previous spreads)
Lights, camera, action:
Valerie's dramatic flair
on fine display.

Valerie is a genius at
achieving proportion,
and a master at playing
with textures and form.

white shirts she still cherishes, especially his
very first lazier cut batistes.

After the tragedy of losing her young son,
her mother, and her husband all in the span
of a year, she went underground and became
almost invisible, dedicating her life to the
foundation and helping other mothers. She
became a national speaker, raising money to
fund the foundation that she started with her
own money. After sixteen years of mourning,
her sorrow lifted while she was on sabbatical.
Coming out at the other end transformed her
and when she re-emerged, it was with aban-
donment, as if compensating for the dark
years. Now, her "desire is to celebrate what
there is still left to celebrate" and this can be
seen in her sartorial choices.

Whether Valerie is wearing the elevated
designs of Lanvin, Céline, or Tomas Maier,
or the complex confections of Comme des
Garçons, Junya Watanabe, or John Galliano,
or an emerging designer, she is daring and
devil-may-care. She embraces retailers like
Opening Ceremony and delights in the
relatively unknown new designers who she
passionately supports. The young genius
of Aliona Kononova, Jerell Scott, and Andrew
Morrison are dear to her.

Valerie's ensembles are always unique,
charming, and downright playful. She is never
"worn by her clothes," refusing to "sacrifice
either femininity or attractiveness for the sake
of fashion." Rather, she puts her own spin on it
and spin she does. It is this whimsical approach
to dressing that I most admire about her, this
woman who has lived through so much. Valerie
never takes herself too seriously. She has fun
with her clothes. Yes, all heads turn when she
enters a room; more importantly, all hearts
melt when she opens her mouth.

Adding pencils to a
vintage jacket adds just
the right touch of whimsy,
echoing the texture of
the oversized knit hat.

(opposite)
The veil on the hat adds
mystique, intrigue and
a sense of class.

160

ENRICA CARRETTI

Enrica loves contrast and way before
it was a trend, she would wear sneakers
with her gowns.

Timeless elegance: Enrica
exudes it in spades.

Enrica Carretti

I first met Enrica Carretti in the Garage, a venerable spot in New York City, which during the week served as a parking garage and on the weekends was transformed into a flea market. Known as the place to go to score endless antique treasures and amazing finds, it attracted thousands of locals and tourists from all over the world who faithfully made the trek to twenty-fourth Street and Sixth Avenue every Saturday and Sunday, getting there as early as 6 a.m. to find the best deals. It was there that I first laid eyes on this Italian beauty and stopped dead in my tracks to find out more. Yes, it was her looks and style that first attracted me, but it was also the fierce sense of self and presence that she exuded. I wanted to know her immediately. We exchanged phone numbers and our friendship was sealed right then and there.

Enrica was born in Correggio, a town in the Emilia-Romagna region of Italy, the birthplace of the Renaissance painter Antonio Allegri, who was called "il Correggio." Influenced by her beautiful mother and elegant grandfather, who both took great pride in their appearance and aimed for perfection in their dress, young Enrica was the only one in her town to wear clothes that stood out and that she chose herself (unlike other girls her age whose mothers chose their outfits). Encouraged by her mother, who still today at the age of eighty dresses in an ever-changing array of colorful and beautiful clothes that she delights in, Enrica's love of clothing and design began early. She went to an artistic high school and graduated with honors from the University of Bologna, the oldest university in the western world, with a degree in Italian Literature and History of Art and went on to earn a PhD in Marketing,

Communication, and Advertising from the University of Reggio Emilia.

It is art that informs Enrica's style and aesthetic. Her wardrobe consists of elegant, well-made pieces that she pairs with ethnic textiles and accessories. She chooses items that speak to her, and to the artist in her, and that resonate with her being. She loves contrast and, way before it was a trend, she was wearing sneakers with her gowns. When her hair started to grow grey, Enrica chose to go natural rather than be a slave to color. Today she has a gorgeous head full of black hair with elegant grey streaks throughout.

Enrica exudes confidence and strength and her goal is to design clothes that imbue the wearer with these traits. A designer for an Italian company that offers quality clothes and accessories for the larger woman, Enrica is happiest when she sees a client come out of a dressing room wearing a dress that shows off her curves, and which she originally may have thought was not for her. Often both are moved to tears by witnessing the excitement and confidence that well-fitting and well-made clothes can impart. Enrica's goal is to democratize fashion, believing that fashion is for every woman, not just the skinny ones. This is the challenge Enrica faces in her design work and meeting it gives her immense satisfaction. She follows the philosophy that style is timeless. "Forget trends, find your own style, wear what you love, be proud of who you are, and be yourself," she says. She admires Coco Chanel, who she considers the most important woman in the history of fashion.

For our interview, we meet at the Maritime Hotel, where she is staying. She is all

(opposite)
The juxtaposition
between the finely
embroidered dress
and the oversized
jade neck piece hits
just the right notes
of interest and art.

packed, ready to leave for the airport in an hour. Yet she happily agrees to unpack the suitcase and show us her clothes. Enrica wears classic pieces that travel well, wear well, and are suited for every occasion and city in the world. She mixes these timeless pieces with gorgeous bold accessories and the occasional vintage piece, such as the striking vintage Japanese fireman's coat that she picked up at a flea market in Los Angeles. Paired with her black and white sneakers, she is as elegant in this outfit as in her gorgeous Max Mara textured dress or

classic green coat. As we pass through the busy hotel's lobby to go out for our photo shoot, every head turns to admire the beauty that just whizzed by. Yes, ladies, sit up and take notice and learn from this master teacher.

Combining an antique
Japanese fireman's
coat with pearls and
Adidas makes this outfit
effortlessly chic and
forever cool.

Enrica Carretti

TERRI
WONG

The garments Terri chooses to put
on her body reflect her values: kindness,
love, harmony, balance, beauty.

We meet Terri in her house in the Sunset district of San Francisco. Sunny and spacious, filled with traditional Chinese furniture, orchids, and plants everywhere, as well as books, artworks, and five birds nestled in their bird cages, this is a well-attended home. She leads us into her bedroom, where a traditional Chinese embroidered robe is hanging on the door, and begins showing us her treasures: exquisite traditional coats and jackets, beautifully hand-embroidered using the forbidden stitch pattern (named after the Forbidden City, where it was invented for the Imperial court; the stitch resembles a small knot with a dimple in its center). She opens her closet to reveal colorful embroidered and beaded sweaters from the fifties, cropped silk cigarette pants in an array of colors, and 124 pairs of shoes.

The shoes are works of art, really; small sculptures that Terri has amassed over the years at various antique stores and fairs. Her tiny feet—size 4—are happily encased in a variety of whimsical flights of fancy, shoes of bygone days when form and function resulted in beautifully crafted and surprisingly comfortable and wearable creations. Next, she shows us her hats, a collection of Chinese children's hats with pom-poms and bats, colorful, playful, imaginative delights. Many she has crocheted herself and finished off with antique trim that she buys at Britex, a San Francisco treasure trove for antique trims and fabrics.

Terri's huge bakelite bracelet collection is displayed on bracelet forms, and in intricate carved boxes sit her hundreds of pairs of vintage earrings. There are numerous necklaces and bracelets of jade, her favorite stone. The bed is covered with an antique Chinese embroidered bedspread; everywhere in her home is evidence of beautiful handwork.

Terri's family is from mainland China. It was traditional for girls to learn sewing in school and needlework was a way for women to make money outside the home. Her grandmother tried to teach her granddaughter these skills, but Teri's sewing skills proved disastrous, so Grandma sent her to knitting lessons instead, which proved fortuitous. Growing up with an abusive mother, knitting was a way for young Terri to ground herself. She went on to study opera and during rehearsals she and the other singers were always doing something with their hands: quilting, knitting, weaving. To this day, Terri's hands are never idle—she continually has her knitting bag with her and thinks nothing of taking out whatever project she is working on whenever and wherever a spare moment presents itself. At the age of nineteen, Terri discovered Buddhism and the combination of spirituality and knitting helped her to overcome an eating disorder and to lead a richly productive, creative life. Terri is the proud mother of a daughter, Mariko, and she celebrates life by giving to others gifts from her heart: handmade items such as a sweater, a home-cooked meal, or even a song.

As the canaries serenade us, we sit down to a sumptuous lunch of Chinese buns with Terri's homemade pickles, sautéed greens and tea. Terri is equally at home in the kitchen as she is in her studio with her knitting, crocheting, or restoration work. The day of our visit she is dressing for the opening of the Tribal Antique Show, an annual vintage fair held in San Francisco. She wears

(opposite)
Sisters at heart:
wearing our respective
Chinese hats.

a late nineteenth-century celadon Chinese
robe she restored herself, featuring colorful
embroidered roosters on the front and
back, and a bat, her totem, on the right back
shoulder. The blue cuffs are decorated with
silver-embroidered foo dogs. She pairs it with
vintage magenta silk capri pants with beaded
cuffs from Ann Taylor. Around her neck is
a serpentine and copal necklace by San Francisco jeweler Masha Archer. On her head is
a late nineteenth-century Chinese child's hat
with a phoenix on top. On her feet are vintage
magenta open-toe springolator pumps.

The next day we meet to go to Chinatown
to visit her favorite tea bar. Terri is again
dressed in an impeccable mix of collectible

vintage pieces, her own hand-knit accessories,
and contemporary brands. She is a lady.

Terri's style perfectly suits her: slim pants;
feminine sweaters that show off a woman's
curves; beautifully hand-embroidered
Chinese coats to reflect her heritage and
her love and devotion to handwork and
craft. Her choices in the garments she puts
on her body reflect her values: kindness, love,
harmony, balance, beauty. Terri's outer self
reflects her inner self, revealing a woman
with enormous respect for the arts, for hu-
manity, and for the treasures of the heart.

Terri's collection
of antique Chinese
hand-embroidered
children's hats.

(opposite)
Antique hand-embroi-
dered Chinese coat.

179   Terri Wong

Chinese hand-embroidered jacket worn with a bespoke necklace made of antique Chinese pieces, worn with a jade ring and antique bracelet.

(opposite)
Hat by Masha Archer, earrings by Sally Bass, and vintage sunglasses. Note the pop of the unexpected blue scarf tied at the neck.

180

Terri wearing a hat she
embellished herself with
peacock feathers.

(opposite)
A detail of fine hand
embroidery on one of
Terri's many Chinese
children's hats.

RUTH
SHUMAN

Ruth's dynamic style reflects her life's work of bringing color and art to underserved New York City public schools.

(previous spread)
The lady of color wearing a
Prada skirt, and a Gaetano
Pesce ring and bracelet.

Born in Montreal to a prominent Jewish Canadian family, Ruth Shuman was influenced by parents who cared about living with beautiful things and grandparents who owned an exquisite house. Ruth's aesthetic is immediately felt and seen when you walk into her apartment where a profusion of color, art, form, and design greets you, immediately putting a smile on your face.

Designed by her longtime friend, the well-known Italian designer Gaetano Pesce, the space is filled with his highly original and playful works. It's clearly an ode to the uplifting effects of color and art, a fitting home for the woman who founded Publicolor, an organization that runs educational programs for at-risk kids, including its flagship program that enlists students to help transform New York's lowest-performing schools by painting stairwells, cafeterias, and corridors in bright and cheerful colors.

Ruth studied art history at the University of Pennsylvania and went on to study industrial design at Pratt Institute, which she found so exciting that she continued to take courses for the next twelve years. She became involved with the Big Apple Circus in its infancy, doing whatever it took to help promote it and loving every second of her involvement. This is a woman who "does," a woman who takes action, a woman who makes things happen, a woman with a mission, a woman with passion and a huge heart. It was after her first visit to a public school, where she saw the grey walls and dismal surroundings, that she got the idea to transform an "environment of disrespect" to one that instead empowers and enriches the lives of its students. She founded Publicolor in 1996 with her own funds and today it's one of the twelve recipients of the National Arts and Humanities Youth Program. Publicolor is grounded in research showing that changing an environment can change attitudes and behavior. At its heart, Publicolor engages underserved students in their own education by using color, collaboration, and design. Over the years, Publicolor has transformed more than four hundred struggling schools and under-resourced community facilities, such as homeless shelters and local health and community centers, into cheerful, colorful oases.

So what does a woman wear who heads such an impactful organization all about color and art? "Prada," she tells me, which is no surprise since its designer, Miuccia Prada, is influenced by art and architecture, choosing architects such as Rem Koolhaas to design the New York flagship store and Herzog & de Meuron to design the Tokyo store. Ruth also favors the clothes of the Japanese designers, such as Issey Miyake, known for his technology-driven designs, and Yohji Yamamoto, known for his avant-garde tailoring. Ruth typically pairs these clothes with bracelets and rings by Pesce, ensuring her sartorial choices reflect her life's work of bringing color and art to all those lucky enough to come in contact with this walking dynamo.

Ruth keeps it simple with
a black sweater on top
and goes for a pop of color
with the embroidery on
the Prada skirt, adding
texture and interest with
the Gaetano Pesce ring
and the Tone Vigeland
bracelet.

Ruth keeps it interesting
with a pop of color on the
embellishment of the dress,
and adds texture with her
bracelets and rings.

(opposite)
If it's not broken, don't fix
it. Ruth stays true to her
aesthetics in a simple black
top by Yohji Yamamoto,
a colorful and playful
Comme des Garçons skirt,
colorful flat shoes and
a signature bracelet.

MARJORIE STERN

"Be emboldened, have courage, take a chance, develop your own style."

Marjorie wearing a
vintage Kansai jacket.
This is the jacket she wore
when Bill Cunningham
first approached her,
delighted by her vision.

Born and raised in New York City, Marjorie
Stern has New York in her blood, pulsating
with the beat of the city, its nonstop energy,
its creativity. She attended Carnegie Tech
Theater School and ultimately got her BA
in theater from New York University School
of Drama. A firm believer that you do whatever it takes to get the job, and then figure
it out as you go along, Marjorie has had a
multifaceted career, from running her own
mail-order company and being the catalog
coordinator at Bergdorf Goodman to owning
multiple accessory stores. For the past ten
years she has owned an upscale children's
store on the Upper West Side called A Time
for Children where 100 percent of the profit
is donated to the Children's Aid Society of
New York. A number of the youth are enrolled
in year-round training programs in which
they learn about retail sales, merchandising,
and buying. The teenagers work in the store
for six months and are then placed in jobs
elsewhere.

Consummate New Yorkers, Marjorie and
her husband are both passionate about
giving back to the city they love. Although
strictly not-for-profit, Marjorie attends to
her store as though her livelihood depended
on it. In fact, it was while she was on the
way to the office that we first met, on the
corner of 57th Street and 5th Avenue, where
Bill Cunningham would stand on the lookout
for stylish New Yorkers. One day we both
stopped to say hello to Bill as he snapped
away, and sensing we were kindred spirits, a
friendship easily ensued.

Marjorie's sartorial choices stem from her
desire to express her individuality and her
highly evolved sense of aesthetics and style.
The same artistic expression presents itself
in her clothing, in her apartment, in the way
she sets a table. Never one to follow trends or
wear what others are wearing, Marjorie prefers to shop in off-the-beaten-path boutiques
such Opening Ceremony and Dover Street
Market and prefers cutting-edge designers
such as Junya Watanabe, Yohji Yamamoto,
Comme des Garçons, Issey Miyake—Japanese
designers she has favored for decades and
whose pieces she has kept since they first
came on the scene. As she shows us her
incredible wardrobe—a white coat by Henrik
Vibskov; a Misty Harbor raincoat hand-painted with the likeness of Superman, Spider-Man,
and Batman by Suzan Pitt; a multicolored
Kansai Yamamoto coat that she has had
since the eighties (which I so understand as
I still wear his pants that I've had since then);
a short-sleeved silver coat by Gareth Pugh;
a plaid Comme des Garçons cutaway; a pink
feathered coat by William Ivey Long that
belonged to her dear friend Joan Rivers; a
coat made of large silver payettes that Joan
had made for her—all paired with slim black
pants and flat boyish shoes—you understand
why she was one of Bill's favorite subjects
and was consistently in his style columns.

This is a woman who is not afraid to be
different, to stand out, to make statements.
She encourages others to do the same:
"Be emboldened, try something different,
don't pay attention to what others say, take
risks, have courage, take a chance, develop
your own style." Whether at the opening
night of the opera or at trade shows buying
merchandise for her store, or on her way
to work, Marjorie is always a vision to behold,
impossible not to notice, and always true
to who she is. New York is truly blessed to
call her one of its own.

Marjorie's love of texture
is seen here in her Gareth
Pugh silver coat layered
with strings of necklaces
collected over the years.

(previous page)
Marjorie's love of the
whimsical is seen here
in her Misty Harbor
raincoat, hand-painted
by Suzan Pitt with
Superman, Spider-Man
and Batman.

More texture seen here
in this white cut-out coat
by Henrik Vibskov.

CARMEN DE LAVALLADE

"You are always playing a role. 'All the world is a stage,' is true. Be conscious of your appearance. You want to look sharp. You want to look respectful."

Carmen de Lavallade was born in East Los Angeles to Creole parents from New Orleans. She was raised by her Aunt Adele, who owned one of the first African-American bookshops and was surrounded by three other aunties, one of whom taught her how to sew. A huge influence on young Carmen was her cousin Janet Collins, the first African-American prima ballerina in the Metropolitan Opera. Carmen was inspired to be a dancer like Janet and received a scholarship to study dance with Lester Horton, who became her mentor. She went on as a member of the Lester Horton Dance Theater, where she was a lead dancer.

After many years dancing with Lester Horton, she and her friend Alvin Ailey left for New York to perform in *House of Flowers* on Broadway. It was there that she met her husband, Geoffrey Holder, a choreographer, set and costume designer, and painter who quickly took her under his wing and was to be her greatest champion and biggest fan for the next sixty years, until his death in 2014.

Along with ballet and modern and ethnic dance, throughout her life Carmen has studied other art forms including painting, acting, and set and costume design. Over her long career, Carmen has danced as the prima ballerina in productions at the Metropolitan Opera and was a guest artist at the American Ballet Theatre. She toured Asia with the Alvin Ailey Dance Company, where in some performances the company was billed as the de Lavallade–Ailey American Dance Company. In 1970 she joined the Yale Repertory Theater and taught movement to the actors at the Yale School of Drama. Carmen has had ballets created for her by Alvin Ailey, Agnes de Mille, Glen Tetley, and John Butler.

Her most recent work is her one-woman show, *As I Remember It*, an intimate portrait of her life told through dance, film, and personal writings.

Now in her eighties, she is still performing with an incredible level of grace and elegance. When I ask her about her style, she is quick to respond: "It was all Geoffrey." He made all the costumes for her performances, as well as the dresses she wore to their annual visit to the White House. He would choose the fabric and then design the dresses and have them made by a top costume house in New York. Most of the gowns were cut on the bias, a technique that allows the garment to hug the body and give it form. It also allows for movement, a most needed element both on the dance floor and in life. Geoffrey frequently went to France and would bring back fabric, often in red, Carmen's favorite color. He was always shopping for her, buying her wonderful accessories and fans, orchestrating how she would remove the coat and reveal the gown or dress underneath. He loved petticoats and used them in multitude. Geoffrey adored drama, the theatrics of it all. Carmen was his queen, and regal and majestic she looked. And regal and majestic she felt. With her hair pulled back, her long neck, and small patrician head, Carmen was and still is the epitome of grace and style, both on the stage and off.

Carmen tells me about a book that deeply affected her: *How to Tame a Wild Elephant*, by Jan Chozen Bays, a book about mindfulness. It has helped her to become more aware of her surroundings, more aware of her actions, more aware of her body. "Your body is your servant. It is always working for you. You must respect it."

This leads us into a discussion about the way some actresses dress today. She jumps up to show me a copy of a current magazine that covers celebrities. As she flips through the pages, she grows more adamant. "They dress like the women who used to stand on the street corners. They don't know they are being taken for a ride. There is no respect." We get on the topic of the Metropolitan Museum Gala last year for the opening of the exhibit "China: Through the Looking Glass." "Since when do the Chinese wear no clothes?" she asks, referring to the prolific display of body parts by the actresses and pop stars in attendance. This brings us to one of the most important elements of the art of dressing: occasion.

Carmen is passionate on this subject and the importance of dressing for the particular time and event one is attending. When attending an event at an institution such as the Metropolitan Museum of Art and, in particular, their party of the year, you do your homework. Out of reverence and respect for the host, you show up appropriately dressed. "Keep your mystery," advises Carmen. "Hide behind a fan, give just enough away. Less is best, ladies. It's a game." With clothes, you can leave things to the imagination, that's the excitement. She mentions the Japanese geishas whose kimonos were cut in a precise way to show the nape of the neck, a particularly erotic look.

Take it from a woman who knows, a woman who has been on the world's finest stages and honored by the most prestigious institutions. "You are always playing a role," Carmen says. "'All the world is a stage,' is true. Be conscious of your appearance. You want to look sharp. You want to look respectful."

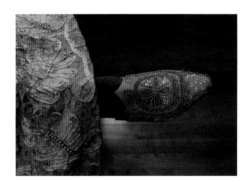

Color, texture, and form: The stuff with which Geoffrey Holder imbued his wife's costumes.

Pattern and color upon pattern and color: the stuff of art.

(previous page)
Because Carmen is short-waisted, Geoffrey lengthened her torso by making the dress waist fall below her actual waist. Dolman sleeves heighten the drama.

Carmen de Lavallade

FROM BERKELEY HIPPIE TO NEW YORK CHIC

How, then, did I go from Berkeley hippie to the chic and sophisticated woman of today? How did I find my style?

The first thing I did was cut my long curly hippie hair into a bob. That single act was a huge transformation. The haircut revealed my cheekbone, my jawline, my long neck, and my finely shaped head—qualities I did not know I possessed. I discovered that I could sleek back my hair and look masculine; indeed, I was then often mistaken for a man when seen from the back. I grew to like the effect and started wearing men's trousers that I bought at Charivari, the men's clothing store where I worked. It was there that I met a woman named Rene Lewis who came in to look at the Claude Montana men's leather jackets.

Rene was a tall woman and a striking presence in her python-leather cowboy boots. The molecules in the air seemed to dance around her. I was instantly drawn to her and pursued her for months. She finally invited me over for tea and that meeting changed my life forever. Her tiny studio apartment was a jewel box filled with Victorian antiques, a brass bed, crystal beaded curtains, Tiffany stained glass hanging in the windows, flowers in beautiful crystal vases, embroidered fringed piano shawls on tables. It was a world I had never seen and one I immediately wanted to inhabit. It was she who introduced me to the world of antiques, and it was her exquisite vintage clothes that no longer fit her, which she gifted me, that started my now extensive antique clothing collection. Rene, a collector from childhood who in her teens set up in flea markets, had an eye like no other and purchased only the best of everything. Just as in my childhood, when I had on my back the finest clothes couturiers could make in the garments my parents sewed for me, and the finest clothes money could buy in the dresses from Neiman Marcus that my aunt sent me, I now had on my back the finest of antique clothes from the Rene Lewis collection. The bar was set very high indeed.

At Barneys, where we were allowed two outfits at 50 percent off, I bought an Armani suit that was a replica of a man's walking suit from the turn of the century. It came with knickers, rather than a skirt or pants, and I discovered that these were the most flattering for my body and suited me well. I could be

creative with the socks and hose I chose to
wear with them and they added another
element of interest to the outfit. I started
viewing dressing as an artist views a painting,
with my body as the blank canvas and the
clothes and accessories as the paints in the
tool box. I slowly realized that, indeed, I
was an artist, only I did not paint, I dressed.

To set my standards, I remembered the
Matisse paintings that I surrounded myself
with in my one-room cottage in Berkeley,
where I would spend hours lying on my bed,
my eyes traveling from one painting to the
next. He was my master, and his use of color,
proportion, and depth sharpened my eyes
into diamonds.

When I started working at Jezebel,
a restaurant decked out in the finest of antiques, I had in my boss, Alberta Wright,
a woman with exceptional style that I could
emulate. I wore vintage dresses and skirts
with silk blouses, favoring Edwardian clothes
from the early teens and twenties. Alberta
encouraged me to wear hats, often bringing
me ones taken from her own closet that were
made by some of the finest milliners: Hattie
Carnegie, Irene of NY, Lilly Daché, Christian
Dior, Mr. John. I discovered I loved hats, that
I looked good in them, and that they were
an easy way to stand out in a crowd and get
noticed. And, of course, I wore only red lipstick. Red lipstick was the color of choice of
all the stylish women I saw and wanted to
emulate. A classic, it shows boldness, daring,
drama. It also happens to work well with my
skin tone and, to this day, a blue-red lip is
what I prefer.

I kept refining my look by observing other
stylish women. I thought nothing of copying,
emulating, stealing ideas from anywhere

I found them. I visited museums and studied
the great masters, looking at portraiture.
I spent days at the Islamic Art section of the
Metropolitan Museum of Art, diving into
their Persian miniatures and carefully scruti-
nizing every detail of the garments on both
the men and women. I returned often to
study the textiles and rugs and ceramics
on display, inhaling the colors, the intricate
patterns, the calligraphy, the sheer beauty.
I turned to art books and spent hours at
the beautiful Rizzoli Bookstore on Fifth Ave
and then on Fifty-seventh Street, leafing
through books on fashion, design, art, and
interiors. I went to every fashion exhibit
at the Metropolitan Museum, FIT, and the
Brooklyn Museum, and would even venture
to Washington, D.C., to the Textile Museum
and the Smithsonian.

I came up with certain rules to follow: buy
the best that I could afford; buy one great
piece, rather than several inferior ones; buy
vintage over designer as it is less expensive
and one-of-a-kind; invest in good shoes and
a great bag; case out every store in the city
before zeroing in on the one piece to buy per
season; befriend one salesperson in every
store I frequent, be loyal to her, and enlist her
help to let me know when things go on sale;
never buy anything that has the designer's
name written all over it; never buy anything
that screams it's the work of a particular
designer—in other words, do not buy the "it"
item of the season; be an original, not a fol-
lower; and only buy the item if I am willing to
travel with it for the rest of my life.

I turned every job into an opportunity to
grow and learn and perfect my look. When
I was hired by the production office of
Tamara, the Broadway show based on the

life of the Art Deco artist Tamara de Lempicka, to pass out leaflets at TKTS where people line up for discounted tickets, I studied her portraits closely and noticed her painstaking attention to detail. When dressing to go out for my double shifts on Saturdays and Sundays, I would carefully consider her motto: "Do not copy. Create a new style." I looked at my outfit through her critical eyes and often, thinking that the earrings or bracelets or other accessories did not quite measure up, I would first go to the flea market to find more suitable replacements. As I handed out flyers about the show, tourists often asked me if I was Tamara, to which I answered, "Yes, in a former lifetime."

When a friend moved to California and left me her bicycle, I gave up wearing skirts and donned only pants, which I thought suited me better in my forties. I was now wearing men's striped pajama bottoms with a great vintage silk blouse or sweater and beautiful vintage fitted jackets, Robert Clergerie shoes, and a Prada bag. Two themes were clearly emerging in my dress: the elegant European woman rooted in the Austrian-Hungarian Empire and the Middle Eastern/Oriental young boy.

I loved looking feminine in beautifully fitted embroidered jackets and pants with a cloche, or other elegant hat, as much as I loved looking like an Orthodox Jewish boy with short pants that ended at the knees, white shirt, black vest, three-quarter-length jacket, and embroidered fez.

The more I honed my look and refined it, the easier it was to shop. I frequented flea markets, antique shows, and vintage stores on a regular basis and my eye would quickly spot the few items that screamed my name. At the same time, the vendors grew to know my style and started putting aside items they thought I would like. Invariably, those items went home with me.

Another revelation was hats and how they completed an outfit. Now, at least three hundred hats later, I wouldn't dream of *not* wearing one. In fact, it is often how an outfit starts—from the hat down. Hats are the exclamation point! The perfect finishing touch to any outfit. They are also whimsical delights that leave a smile on the face of the viewer and are great conversation starters. Hats, as well as other head gear, set you apart, imparting an air of whimsy, playfulness, majesty, and

drama. They are the quickest and easiest way to change your look and your mood and with them there is never a bad hair day!

In my fifties, after my inner spiritual transformation that allowed me to claim my identity as a dresser, my style blossomed. I discovered antique Chinese robes, with their finely embroidered peonies on exquisite silk fabric that made my heart swoon. I was smitten and quickly started acquiring as many of these as my wallet would allow. At the time, Asia Week New York was a yearly occurrence, bringing with it vendors who specialized in these robes. Although quite pricey, the dealers were willing to work out payment plans wth me. I was soon wearing Chinese robes exclusively, to the jealousy of the other clothes in my closet that somehow no longer made the cut. A few years later, a new friend introduced me to the world of the geishas and I started acquiring antique Japanese kimonos. I was being stretched and I welcomed the expansion. "Wear what you love, and the world will love what you wear" has been a motto I try to live by.

"Where do you find your clothes?" I am often asked. The truth is, they find me. Sure, I seek them out, frequenting flea markets, antique fairs, vintage stores, consignment shops, Barneys, and Bergdorf Goodman, but more often than not, somehow the really good vintage pieces come to me. Once, I was at the Pier Antique Show when a woman tapped me on the shoulder and told me she had a cape she thought I would be interested in. I followed her back to her booth and, sure enough, there was the perfect black wool cape—it was voluminous, luxurious, and fit me as though my own father had tailor-made it for me. Another time, I walked into the

CancerCare Thrift Shop and the store's manager told me she was holding a few pieces in the back room for me. To my delight, she had saved an entire collection of antique items delivered by the chauffeur of a wealthy, well-traveled patron. I walked out with two exquisite Japanese kimonos from the 20s, an early Turkmenistan wool coat fully beaded with silver coins, and a '20s hand-embroidered Palestinian cape. Talk about luck. Talk about befriending the sales associates at your favorite stores!

I truly believe that my fairytale childhood growing up dressed in the finery of a princess has set my life's trajectory to attract the finely made garments that I find. My eyes were trained for them and my body is used to the feel of fine silks and velvets and the pleasure of well-fitting custom-made clothes. Set the bar high and the universe will bend to meet your standards. I received confirmation of this a few years ago when I was packing to go to Los Angeles for several months. I assembled all my clothes in front of me—bringing them forth from behind the screen, under the bed, from storage, from the various closets— so that I could see them all. It was an aha moment as I gazed at my museum-quality works of art. How did I acquire these treasures? How was I so fortunate to amass a treasure trove of priceless clothing and textiles? I believe this is what's possible when one's imagination is set free, when one marches to the beat of her own drum, and when one truly delights in the pleasure of dress.

THE KEEPER
OF THE CLOTH

In February 2006, on the first anniversary of my father's death, his first Yahrzeit, as is the custom among Jews, I lit the twenty-four hour memorial candle and went to synagogue. It was a Saturday morning and that Shabbat, the parashah, the weekly Torah portion in the annual Jewish cycle of Torah reading, was Tetzaveh, God's instructions to Moses about making the clothing of Aaron, his brother, the high priest: "Make sacral vestments for Aaron your brother for dignity and adorn-ment." (Exodus, 27:20–30:10)

I was stunned. Being a fervent Jew, but not one well versed in the Torah, I had no idea that such a chapter existed, and certainly one that was so fitting for my father, a hum-ble tailor whose whole life was devoted to achieving that perfect fit. With tears run-ning down my face, I realized this was God's handiwork and that my father's life, and hence mine, was intricately connected to clothing. I wanted to learn more and made an appointment to see the rabbi to glean further the meaning of this parashah. As we sat and read the Hebrew text together, I learned that the words actually say: "you shall instruct all who are skillful, whom I

have endowed with the gift of skill, to make Aaron's vestments, for consecrating him to serve Me as priest." Surely, it was my father, the tailor, whom God was referring to, "en-dowed with the gift of skill." And if it was my father, one of the skillful ones, who was there and made Aaron's vestments then, and since he was the skillful one who made my vestments in this lifetime, then I, in some way, was Aaron, the high priestess, called upon to dress with *kavod* and *tifferet*—honor and splendor, holiness and beauty.

Right then and there, with the rabbi as my witness, I made a vow to dedicate my life to those two principles—dignity and adorn-ment. From that day on, I have come to view my dressing as a holy and sacred act, a calling given to me from on high, one that I have signed up for and one that I am privileged to fulfill to my utmost abilities.

A few years ago, I took on the name "the keeper of the cloth." It called to me, tapped me on the shoulder, and whispered, "take me on, own me, bring me to life." The title seemed to fit perfectly with my growing understanding of my life's work, a calling I realized first when two rabbis acknowledged

The antique Turkman cuff on my wrist is my favorite bracelet. I bought it in Jerusalem, in one of the shops across from the King David Hotel, while I was on my way to the post office to convert the $400 in cash in my pocket to a money order to send to my landlord in New York. Needless to say, the rent was a bit late that summer. A girl must have her priorities straight.

my dressing. I've come to realize that I'm committed to garments with a past—of the past—with a story to tell, and a history to impart. As a storyteller who tells stories with her clothes, my love of antique pieces, and specifically handmade, hand-embroidered, and finely rendered clothing is an integral part of who I am. It's why I devote so much of my time, energy, and hard-earned money to seek out these clothes, alter them, and repair them time and time again.

I am my mother's and my father's daughter; the product of two terrifically skilled artisans whose hands could do anything and everything with cloth. Given that such is my heritage and that from my beginnings I was swathed in clothing fit for a princess, I can do no less than uphold their standards. In these antique clothes, I find the craftsmanship and quality that I am used to. Let others go for the newest, the latest, the sexiest. I will forever be collecting and wearing and attending to the clothes of the past and I will forever be grateful for the honor of being the keeper of the cloth.

DEDICATION

Unbeknown to us, while Bill and I were perched on our bicycles talking, and he was taking a photo of me, a passerby snapped our picture. The next day a friend of mine found it on the internet and sent it to me. I will forever treasure it.

BILL CUNNINGHAM

It was my hope that Bill Cunningham would write the foreword to this book. With his untimely death, this was not meant to be. Instead, here I am, with tears in my eyes, writing about him. Perhaps this is exactly as it should be because it is, after all, Bill who made this book possible in the first place. Let me explain.

In the winter of 2013, I was in Paris for my first Fashion Week. As I had been one of the models in Lanvin's 2012 fall/winter campaign, I was invited to attend their fashion show. Bill was thrilled to see me there and when he spotted me from across the bleachers he stood up and waved and motioned for me to meet him downstairs. With the grin of a child, he hugged and kissed me, so happy that I had finally made it to the City of Lights. In spite of the freezing weather and the snow falling on our faces, we stood outside while he snapped my photo and chatted away. The next day, I was exploring the city, and sure enough, there he was. We stopped to talk and he asked me what other shows I was attending. When I told him I was not invited to any, he shook his head and said, "Oh, no, child, we must fix that." He promptly reached into his

bag and pulled out two invites he was not going to be able to use and handed them to me. One was for the Vivienne Westwood show, which was to start in an hour. He directed me to how to get there and sent me off on my merry way. I was thrilled to be seated in the front row, along with the other reporters and editors from all over the world. Sure enough, the woman next to me, the editor of *New York* magazine, wanted to know who I was and what I was doing in Bill's seat. When I explained, she inquired as to what I do and I told her that I hold seminars called "The Art of Dressing," in which I use my clothes to teach the principles of design and style. She asked for my card so that she might send a reporter to write about it. A few weeks later I got an email from her asking when my next seminar was taking place. I quickly put one together and she indeed sent her reporter. When the article in "the Cut" came out, I had several inquiries about my class, including one from a woman in Rhode Island who owns several women's clothing stores. We arrange for me to offer both my one-woman show, *The Fabric of My Life*, and my *Art of Dressing* seminar to her customers and off

Sat. 20 July 2013

Dear Tziporah..... What a grand surprise to see you on Monday. I thought I had lost a prime subject to Los Angeles. and there you were, the news that Calif loves you + appreciated your art & style is thrilling. don't let the New York invite take the glow off. all the good of California. but thanks Tziporah for lifting my spirit this week with your style.
fondly, Bill

The 57th Street gang:
Marjorie Stern, Timothy
John and I would often
meet on the corner of 57th
Street and 5th Avenue
where Bill perched himself
most mornings. He always
broke out in a huge grin
when he saw us coming.

Nothing Gold Can Stay A rare street-fashion vignette, often observed on Fifth Avenue in Midtown, is a group of strangers, attracted by one another's highly individual style of dress, who pause on their way to work to inquire of their clothes. The tradition may vanish, as one member of the group is moving to California. At times, they spontaneously try on one another's look. Last week, nature provided a backdrop only it could create. In Central Park, a "Brigadoon" mist settled over the lake, and cascades of willows framed the Bow Bridge. All over the city, the ginkgo tree proved once again as the leaves fell that Manhattan streets are indeed paved with gold.

ON THE STREET

Updating Capri Pants

Capri or bicycle pants, a look from the 1950's, have returned, and this time around, it's the shoe that makes the difference. Capris evolved from acrobats' tights and came into fashion at the end of World War II. Originally worn with Capezio flats, they are being worn today with an eclectic range of footwear: platform clogs and other backless styles, chunky sneakers, delicate evening designs, 40's wedgies and 50's pumps.

ST 5

Van Cleef & Arpels

...what was manufactured to catch his eye, but what people wore to telegraph their pl...

The photo on the bottom where only my legs and shoes are shown was the first time I appeared in Bill's column. He was doing a story on mules.

I still often pass 57th Street and 5th Avenue looking for Bill. And yes, I still dress for Bill. And for my parents. And foremost, I DRESS FOR MYSELF!

I went to Providence, where I performed my show on the stage of Rhode Island School of Design and my class in the Clad In Outlet. It was there that I met Jane Lahr, a book agent, who signed me on and pitched the book to Rizzoli, which wanted to publish it. Like a domino effect, because of the invitation that Bill so generously and graciously offered me, you, dear reader, are now reading this book.

I first met Bill Cunningham in front of Bergdorf Goodman in 1990 when my father started working in the alterations department. I was working in a restaurant in the neighborhood so I visited him often, usually after my lunch shift. Bill was there most afternoons with his camera, shooting the passersby who caught his eye for his "On the Street" column in the Sunday *New York Times* Style section. He invariably took my picture. And we started to talk. I told him about my father, about my childhood, about my love of clothes and dressing. Our exchanges became longer and a friendship and love quickly developed. Sometimes as he would be taking my photo, zeroing in on my shoes or a detail on my outfit, I would say, "Hello, Bill," and he would look up and say, "Oh, it's you, child," breaking out in a huge grin.

Bill had a child-like enthusiasm that was infectious. He genuinely loved what he did, loved his subjects, and loved creativity in all its forms. We would often look at the Bergdorf windows together and he would give me his opinion of them. He particularly loved and appreciated their Christmas windows and would be in raptures pointing out their minute details. His knowledge of clothing and fashion history was encyclopedia-worthy. He would look at one of my hats and know exactly when it was made and often the designer who made

it. He would study my jacket or cape and say, "That's from 1939," and then correct himself, "no, 1937." Over the years, we would see each other at art openings or museums and my picture would appear in his "Evening Hours" column. On some blessed occasions, we would run into each other on our bikes, as we made our way through the city. Then, we would stop, bike to bike, so happy that fate had brought us together.

Bill knew of my struggle to find meaning in my work and to figure out what I was meant to do with my gifts and he encouraged me to keep doing what I was doing. He often sent me handwritten letters, thanking me for "soaring his spirits upon seeing me on the Avenue."

In the past few years, life no longer took me to Fifty-seventh Street and Fifth Avenue on a regular basis so I would make an effort to get there as often as I could. Bill would snap away as I disembarked from my bicycle and lingered a few minutes, talking to Marjorie Stern, who always walked by on her way to work, and Timothy John, the artist, who often joined us. We became a family and readily took in anyone else passing by whose style caught Bill's eye. That was the thing about Bill—he was democratic, he was real, he was one of the people. He hated snobbery or pretense of any kind and found beauty everywhere he looked. More than anything, he loved the unique, the eccentric, the one who dares to dress out of the box. He was disappointed that the world had become so cookie-cutter similar in its approach to dress and applauded and showcased individualism, eccentricity, and artistry.

I would like to think he would have loved this book.

ACKNOWLEDGMENTS

This book came to be because of many people.

First and foremost, I owe this book to my parents. It is they who started me off on my lifelong love affair with clothes and adornment. It is their mastery that allowed me to know and experience the joys of dressing. It is their love and support that sustained me throughout the years and gives me sustenance today. Right behind them is my Doda Yoli, my aunt in America, who generously and tirelessly sent us those packages from Neiman Marcus, those gorgeous clothes that kept coming and coming. To my sister Vera, who to this day is my biggest advocate and greatest champion. To Lucie Porges, who saw in me what I could not see in myself and who first suggested that I teach her design students by "bringing the outfits." To Tante Vivian, who encouraged me to be a writer.

I have already mentioned Bill Cunningham, but let me thank him here, as well, for his friendship, generosity of spirit, and big heart. To *New York* magazine for writing the story about my Art of Dressing Seminars and for Elizabeth Day Lawrence, who read the article and hired me to teach it at her wonderful stores Clad In. To Jane Lahr, my agent, who found me at Clad In and who, along with Lyn DelliQuadri, her partner, took me on. Without Jane and Lyn this book would not have been. They believed in it, fought for it, and helped make it happen. To the Rizzoli team, a dream of a publishing company, especially my editor Ellen Nidy, whose guidance and help made my job easy. To Jeanette Abbink, the designer of the book, whose vision, aesthetics, and genius made this book the beauty that it is.

To all the amazingly talented photographers who contributed their work, especially Janis Wilkins, who went with me to every interview and who traveled with me to California and who was on board from the start. To Mokshini, the brilliant illustrator whose whimsical illustrations add a whole other dimension to the book.

To Chuck Citrin and Mary Pleshette Willis who gave me the pep talks I needed to finally take pen in hand. To Henry Aldebot, my doorman, who takes such good care of me. To all the women who have taken my seminars and for all who have not and have asked for a book like this, this is for you.

For Ari Seth Cohen, who started the Advanced Style movement and who featured me in his documentary of the same name.

For Alan Manson, the brother who keeps me together, who has listened to every word, every complaint, and who lightens the load by somehow finding me the perfect shoe. Thank you to my brothers—Phillip Retzky, who loved me when I could not love myself; Bernard Grenier, for putting my home together again and again; for Zachy Sherif, my rock, my Nazo, my twin who stretches me, inspires me, and is my best playmate.

To all the vendors and antique dealers who helped make my wardrobe happen, who put things aside for me, held items for me, and worked with me, wanting me to have the garments as much as I did.

And, of course, to the women of this book, who opened their homes to me, their hearts and their closets, and shared of themselves so generously. It is they who inspire me by leading such exemplary lives and proving that style is an inner job and comes about as a result of love and devotion. With much gratitude to all.
—Tziporah

All illustrations by
Mokshini

Photography

Janis Wilkins
Pages: 58; 59; 70; 71; 74; 75,
upper left; 90; 91; 94; 95; 98; 99;
107; 109; 112; 114; 115; 116-117;
118-119; 120; 121; 123; 124-125; 129;
130; 135; 138; 140-141; 150; 158;
159; 160; 161; 163; 164; 165; 168;
169; 170; 171; 173; 176; 177; 178; 179;
180; 181; 182; 183; 185; 188; 189;
190; 191; 192; 195; 196; 197; 200;
201; 202; 203; 204; 205; 207; 211;
212; 213; 214; 215; 222; 227; 239

Ellin Anderegg
Pages: 132; 133

Iris Brosch
Pages: 39; 218; Front Cover

Gilbert Carrasquillo
 Getty Images
Page 139

Gavin Christopher
Pages: 25; 48; 63; 71, lower right

Yaniv Edry
Pages: 20-21; 30-31; 33

Floto + warner
Page 145

Gary Gershoff / Getty Images
Page 143

Melodie Jeng
Pages: 4-5; 6-7; 66; 67; 75, upper
right, lower right; 151; 221; 225;
2332-233; 234-235

Cheryl Koralik
Pages: 14; 15; 16; 17; 43

Danielle Kosan
The New Potato Blog
Pages: 128; 131

Zandy Mangold
Page 236

Julie McCarthy
Pages: 11, 78; 79

Youssef Nabil
Page 32

Cindy Ord / Getty Images
Page 139

Robbie Quinn
Pages: 50-51; 87;
Back Cover

Dan Rous
Pages: 217; 226

Albert Sanchez
Pages: 153; 156; 157

Ike Ude
Pages: 19; 26; 29; 35; 36; 40;
44; 47; 62; 75, lower left; 82;
83; 86; 106

Courtesy, Bill Cunningham
Pages: 229; 230; 231

Courtesy, Gaetano Pesce
Page 193

Courtesy, Michele Oka-Doner
Pages: 148; 149

First published in the
United States of America in
2017 by Rizzoli International
Publications, Inc.
300 Park Avenue South,
New York, NY 10010
www.rizzoliusa.com

© 2017 Rizzoli International
Publications, Inc
© 2017 Tziporah Salamon

Design:
Rational Beauty,
Jeanette Abbink
Design Intern:
María Gabriela Garuz

Rizzoli editor:
Ellen Nidy

Typeset in Domaine Text
and Domaine Sans Display,
designed by Kris Sowersby
and distributed by
Klim Type Foundry.

2017 2018 2019 2020 2021 /
10 9 8 7 6 5 4 3 2 1

ISBN-13: 978-0-8478-4805-8

Library of Congress Control
Number: 2016962843

Printed and bound in Italy

Distributed to the U.S. trade
by Random House